TABLE OF CONTENTS

	PAGE NUMBER
Section 1: Expressions	1
Section 2: Equations and Inequalities	18
Section 3: Introduction to Functions	32
Section 4: Linear Equations, Functions, and Inequalities	49
Section 5: Quadratic Equations and Functions – Part 1	76
Section 6: Quadratic Equations and Functions – Part 2	90
Section 7: Exponential Functions	108
Section 8: Summary of Functions	118
Section 9: One-Variable Statistics	142
Section 10: Two-Variable Statistics	158

All trademarks and product names referred to in this workbook are the property of their respective owners and used solely for educational purposes. Unless stated otherwise, Algebra Nation has no relationship with any of the companies or brands mentioned in this workbook, our videos, or our resources. Algebra Nation does not endorse or have preference for any of the companies or brands mentioned in this workbook.

Section 1: Expressions
Student Learning Plan

Topic Number	Topic Name	Date Completed	Study Expert(s)	Check Your Understanding Score
1	Using Expressions to Represent Real-World Situations			
2	Properties of Exponents			
3	Operations with Rational and Irrational Numbers			
4	Radical Expressions and Expressions with Rational Exponents			
5	Adding Expressions with Radicals and Rational Exponents			
6	More Operations with Radicals and Rational Exponents			
7	Understanding Polynomial Expressions			
8	Operations with Polynomials – Part 1			
9	Operations with Polynomials – Part 2			

What did you learn in this section? What questions do you still have?

Who was your favorite Study Expert for this section? Why?

Practice Book - Section 1: Expressions

1

Section 1 – Topic 1
Using Expressions to Represent Real-World Situations

1. Write each phrase as a mathematical expression.

Phrase	Mathematical Expression
nine increased by a number	
fourteen decreased by a number	
seven less than a number	
the product of nine and a number	
thirty-two divided by a number	
five more than twice a number	
the product of a number and six	
seven divided by twice a number	
three times a number decreased by eleven	
withdrawing $10 every week from an outstanding balance of $400	

2. Joseph tweets 13 times a day. Define each variable and write an algebraic expression to describe the number of posts after any given number of days.

3. Emanuel has 745 pictures in his phone. His memory is getting full, so he starts deleting 20 pictures every day. Define each variable and write an algebraic expression to describe the number of pictures left on his phone after any given number of days.

4. Ashley posts 17 status updates on her Facebook wall each day. Roberto posts 21 status updates on his Facebook wall each day.

   Part A: Define each variable and write an algebraic expression to describe the combined number of posts for Ashley and Roberto after any given number of days.

   Part B: Write an algebraic expression to describe the difference between number of posts for Ashley and Roberto after any given number of days.

5. Tommy posts 11 pictures on Instagram every day. Elizabeth posts 15 pictures on Instagram every day.

   Part A: Define each variable and write an algebraic expression to describe the combined number of posts for Tommy and Elizabeth after any given number of days.

   Part B: After 7 days, how many pictures have Tommy and Elizabeth posted altogether? How do you know?

6. Homer and Bart plan to buy one computer for $499.00 strictly for gaming purposes. Games cost $49.99 each.

   Part A: Define each variable and write an algebraic expression to describe how much they will spend before sales tax, based on purchasing the computer and the number of games.

   Part B: If they purchase one computer and five games, how much do they spend before sales tax?

   Part C: Homer and Bart have friends. They want to purchase extra controllers. Each controller costs $24.99. Use an algebraic expression to describe how much they spend in total (before sales tax) when they purchase one computer, when they purchase any number of games, and when they purchase any number of extra controllers.

   Part D: What would be the total cost, before sales tax, if Homer and Bart purchase one computer, four games, and three extra controllers?

7. Alex and Leandro purchase two matinee movie tickets. A matinee ticket costs $6.50, a drink costs $5.50, and a bag of popcorn costs $6.00. Define each variable and write an algebraic expression to describe how much they spend based on the number of drinks and bags of popcorn they buy. Identify the parts of the expression by underlining the coefficient(s), circling the constant(s), and drawing a box around the variable(s).

8. The local humane society is restocking on cat food to prepare for kitten season. Very young kittens need kitten formula which costs $3.99 per bottle. Older kittens need wet cat food which costs $1.50 per can.

   Part A: Write an algebraic expression to describe how much the humane society will spend preparing for kitten season. Identify the parts of the expression by underlining the coefficient(s), circling the constant(s), and drawing a box around the variable(s).

   Part B: How much money (before tax) will the humane society spend if they buy 30 bottles of kitten formula and 120 cans of wet cat food?

   Part C: If you add a 7% sales tax to the purchase of bottles of kitten formula and cans of wet cat food, how would the algebraic expression in parts A and B change?

Practice Book - Section 1: Expressions

3

9. Create a storyline (word problem) using the following algebraic expressions:

   Part A: $\frac{1,000}{r}$

   Part B: $75 - 3m$

   Part C: $30 + 2d$

10. An airplane is flying at 35,000 feet above sea level. The airplane starts to descend at a rate of 2,500 feet per minute. Let m be the number of minutes. Which of the following expressions describe the height of the airplane after any given number of minutes?

    Ⓐ $2,500 - 35,000m$
    Ⓑ $2,500 + 35,000m$
    Ⓒ $35,000 - 2,500m$
    Ⓓ $35,000 + 2,500m$

Section 1 – Topic 2
Properties of Exponents

1. Simplify the following expressions.

   Part A: $\frac{2x^3y^3}{4y^2} =$

   Part B: $\left(\frac{x^{-8}}{y^{11}}\right)^{-2} =$

   Part C: $\frac{(2x^3)(x^4)^2}{8x^{11}} =$

2. Your neighbor has a square-shaped pool with side lengths of $3a^5$. What is the area of the pool?

3. Bojangles has a rectangular-shaped roof with a width of $6x^2$ feet and a length $12x^3$. What is the area of the roof?

4. Consider each equation. Find the value of m in each equation below. Justify your answer.

   Part A: $(x^m \cdot x^2)^3 (k^3)^5 = x^{21} k^{15}$

   Part B: $x^3 \cdot y^2 \left(\dfrac{x^2 \cdot y^3 \cdot z^m}{z^{-5}}\right) = x^5 y^5 z$

   Part C: $\left(\dfrac{x^8}{yz^5}\right)^m = 1$

5. John buys a water tank from a company that likes to use exponents as dimensions. The tank he buys has the dimensions b^2 by b^4 by $4c^3$. Which of the following expressions represent the volume of the water tank?

   Ⓐ $4b^8 c^3$
   Ⓑ $4b^6 c^3$
   Ⓒ $12b^8 c^3$
   Ⓓ $2b^6 c^3$

6. The dimensions of Peyton and Parker's sandbox are t^2m by t^5 m by $3v^2$ m. One cubic meter of the sandbox contains $3s^{21}$ grains of sand. Which of the following expressions represent the number of grains of sand in the sandbox?

   Ⓐ $27t^{10} v^2 s^{21}$
   Ⓑ $t^{10} v^2 s^{21}$
   Ⓒ $3t^7 v^2 s^{21}$
   Ⓓ $9t^7 v^2 s^{21}$

7. Consider the equation $a^{-3} = \left(\dfrac{1}{a}\right)^5$.
   What value(s) of a make the equation true?

8. Harry, Louis, and Niall are working with exponents. Harry claims $4^2 \cdot 4^5 = 4^{10}$. Louis claims $4^2 \cdot 4^5 = 4^7$. Niall claims $4^2 \cdot 4^5 = 16^7$. Which student has the correct answer? Explain why.

9. Raymond and Rose were working with exponents.

   Part A: Raymond claims that $5^5 * 5^2 = 5^3$. Rose argues that $5^5 * 5^2 = 5^7$. Which one of them is correct? Use the properties of exponents to justify your answer.

   Part B: Raymond claims that $\dfrac{7^9}{7^5} = 7^4$. Rose argues that $\dfrac{7^9}{7^5} = 7^{45}$. Which one of them is correct? Use the properties of exponents to justify your answer.

Practice Book - Section 1: Expressions

Section 1 – Topic 3
Operations with Rational and Irrational Numbers

1. Describe in your own words what it means to say that integers are closed under addition.

2. Describe in your own words what it means to say that integers are not closed under division.

3. Under which of the following operations are integers closed?

   ☐ Addition
   ☐ Subtraction
   ☐ Multiplication
   ☐ Division

4. Complete the following proof to show that the sum of two rational numbers is a rational number.

   Let $a, b, c,$ and d be integers. Let x and y be rational numbers.

Statements	Reasons
1. a, b, c and d are integers, and x and y are rational numbers.	1. Given
2. $x = \frac{a}{b}$ and $y = \frac{c}{d}$	2.
3. $x + y = x + y$	3.
4. $x + y = \frac{a}{b} + \frac{c}{d}$	4.
5.	5. Use rules for addition of fractions (common denominator, add numerators) to write equivalent expression for $\frac{a}{b} + \frac{c}{d}$.
6. $ad + cb$ is an _____.	6. Integers are closed under addition and multiplication.
7. bd is an integer.	7.
8. $\frac{ad+cb}{bd}$ is a _____ number.	8. Definition of rational number.
9. $x + y =$ a rational number.	9.

6

Practice Book - Section 1: Expressions

5. Write an algebraic proof to show that the product of two rational numbers is a rational number.

   Given: x and y are rational numbers.

Statements	Reasons

6. Complete the following proof by contradiction to show that the sum of a rational number and an irrational number is irrational.

   Given: x is a rational number and y is an irrational number.

   Assume that the sum of a rational number and an irrational number is rational.

Statements	Reasons
1. x is a rational number and y is an irrational number.	1. Given
2. $x + y = z$, where z is a rational number.	2. Assumption
3. $x = \frac{a}{b}$ and $z = \frac{c}{d}$, where $a, b, c,$ and d are integers.	3.
4. $\frac{a}{b} + y = \frac{c}{d}$	4.
5. $y = \frac{c}{d} - \frac{a}{b}$	5.
6.	6. Used rules adding fractions to write equivalent expression for $\frac{c}{d} - \frac{a}{b}$.
7.	7.
8. $cb - ad$ is an _____.	8. Integers are closed under multiplication and subtraction.
9. db is an integer.	9.
10. $\frac{ay-xb}{by}$ is a _____ number.	10.

   We have proven that our assumption is _____. Therefore, the sum of a rational and irrational number must be _____.

Practice Book - Section 1: Expressions

7. Write a proof by contradiction to show that the product of a rational number and irrational number is irrational.

   Given: x is a rational number and y is an irrational number.

Statements	Reasons

8. Based on the previous information, conjecture whether each statement is ALWAYS true, SOMETIMES true, or NEVER true. Circle the correct answer below each statement.

   i. The sum of a rational number and a rational number is rational.

       ALWAYS   SOMETIMES   NEVER

   ii. The sum of a rational number and an irrational number is irrational.

       ALWAYS   SOMETIMES   NEVER

   iii. The sum of an irrational number and an irrational number is irrational.

       ALWAYS   SOMETIMES   NEVER

   iv. The product of a rational number and a rational number is rational.

       ALWAYS   SOMETIMES   NEVER

   v. The product of a rational number and an irrational number is irrational.

       ALWAYS   SOMETIMES   NEVER

   vi. The product of an irrational number and an irrational number is irrational.

       ALWAYS   SOMETIMES   NEVER

9. Does either item below contradict the statement: *"The sum of two rational numbers is a rational number"*?

   Item 1: $\frac{1}{2} + \frac{3}{4} = \frac{5}{4}$

   Item 2: $\frac{1}{2} + \frac{3}{2} = 2$

   (A) Item I contradicts the statement. Item II is an example when the statement is true.
   (B) Item II contradicts the statement. Item I is an example when the statement is true.
   (C) Both Item I and Item II contradict the given statement.
   (D) Neither Item I nor Item II contradicts the given statement.

Practice Book - Section 1: Expressions

10. Select all of the following expressions that result in rational number.

    ☐ $\sqrt{49} - \sqrt{16}$
    ☐ $\sqrt{5} + \sqrt{6} + \sqrt{7} + \sqrt{8}$
    ☐ $10\pi - \pi\sqrt{100}$
    ☐ $(\pi - \sqrt{3})(\pi + \sqrt{3})$
    ☐ $\sqrt{11} - 4$
    ☐ $\pi^2 + 5$
    ☐ $r + s$, where r and s are irrational numbers

11. Thomas argues that $\frac{\sqrt{27}}{\sqrt{3}}$ is rational. Mateo argues that the quotient between $\sqrt{27}$ and $\sqrt{3}$ is irrational. Prove who is right. Make sure you justify your answer.

12. The traffic warning sign below has a triangle shape with base of 18 inches.

    The value of the area of the triangle (half base times altitude), in square inches, is an irrational number. The number that represents the altitude of the triangle must be _____. Select the best answer to fill in the blank.

    Ⓐ A whole number
    Ⓑ A rational number
    Ⓒ An irrational number
    Ⓓ A non-real complex number

    Explain your answer.

Section 1 – Topic 4
Radical Expressions and Expressions with Rational Exponents

1. The following expression shows a simplification of a radical with a missing index.

$$\sqrt[n]{54 \cdot x^6 \cdot y^{12}} = 3x^2 y^4 \sqrt[n]{2}$$

   What is the index n for this expression?

   Ⓐ 2
   Ⓑ 3
   Ⓒ 6
   Ⓓ 9

2. Simplify the expression, $\left(\left(p^{-2} + \frac{1}{p}\right)^1\right)^p$, when $p = \frac{3}{4}$, in both radical and rational exponents forms.

   Radical form:

   Rational exponent form:

Practice Book - Section 1: Expressions

9

3. Write an equivalent expression in rational exponent form.

   Part A: $\sqrt[8]{5^6}$

   Part B: $\sqrt[4]{x^{\frac{2}{3}}}$

   Part C: $\sqrt[3]{8}(\sqrt{8^2}+8^2)$

4. Determine the value of n such that $\sqrt[4]{64^{\frac{1}{3}}}=64^{\frac{1}{n}}$.

5. Determine whether each expression is equivalent to $x^{\frac{7}{4}}$.

Expression	Yes	No
$\sqrt[7]{x^4}$	○	○
$\sqrt[4]{x^7}$	○	○
$(\sqrt[4]{x})^7$	○	○
$\sqrt{x^{\frac{7}{4}}}$	○	○
$\sqrt[4]{x^5} \cdot \sqrt[4]{x^2}$	○	○
$\sqrt[5]{x^4} \cdot \sqrt[2]{x^4}$	○	○
$\dfrac{(\sqrt[4]{x})^7}{(\sqrt{x})^0}$	○	○

6. Write an equivalent expression to $3^{\frac{2}{3}} \cdot \sqrt[8]{3^4}$.

7. Prove that $\left(\dfrac{\sqrt[3]{512x^6y^9}}{\sqrt{16x^4y^6}}\right)^{\frac{1}{2}} = \sqrt{2}$.

10

Practice Book - Section 1: Expressions

Section 1 – Topic 5
Adding Expressions with Radicals and Rational Exponents

1. Perform the following operations and write the answers in radical form.
   Part A: $\sqrt{7} + \sqrt{3} + \sqrt{98} - \sqrt{18}$

   Part B: $3\sqrt{5} - 3\sqrt{11} + 2\sqrt{121} - 3\sqrt{90}$

2. Perform the following operations and write the answers in radical form.
   Part A: $8^{\frac{1}{2}} + 16^{\frac{1}{4}} - 12^{\frac{1}{2}} + 81^{\frac{1}{4}}$

   Part B: $8 \cdot 2^{\frac{1}{2}} - 24^{\frac{1}{4}} - 3^{\frac{1}{2}} + 128^{\frac{1}{4}}$

3. Which of the following expressions are equivalent to $7\sqrt{5}$?
   - ☐ $14^{\frac{1}{2}} \cdot 25^{\frac{1}{2}}$
   - ☐ $49^{\frac{1}{2}} \cdot 5^{\frac{1}{2}}$
   - ☐ $\sqrt{70}$
   - ☐ $\sqrt{155}$
   - ☐ $\sqrt{7} \cdot \sqrt{5}$
   - ☐ $\frac{\sqrt{196} \cdot \sqrt{5}}{2}$
   - ☐ $\frac{\sqrt{49} + \sqrt{25}}{5}$

4. Which of the following expressions are equivalent to $4\sqrt{3}$?
   - ☐ $4^{\frac{1}{3}} + 3^{\frac{1}{3}}$
   - ☐ $27^{\frac{1}{2}} + 3^{\frac{1}{2}}$
   - ☐ $\sqrt{32}$
   - ☐ $\sqrt{48}$
   - ☐ $2\sqrt{12}$
   - ☐ $2\sqrt{18}$
   - ☐ $\sqrt{27} + \sqrt{3}$

5. Prove that $\sqrt{8} + \sqrt{2} = 3 \cdot 2^{\frac{1}{2}}$

6. Find the perimeter of the following figures and circle the figure with the greatest perimeter.

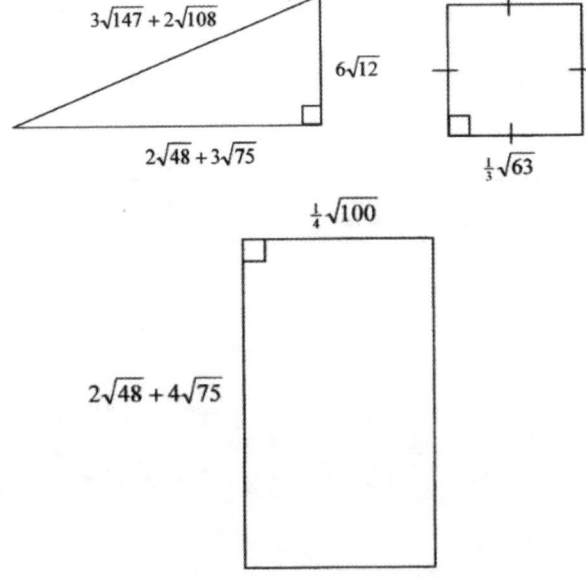

Section 1 – Topic 6
More Operations with Radicals and Rational Exponents

1. Perform the following operations and write the answers in radical form.
   Part A: $(2\sqrt{7} + \sqrt{27})(\sqrt{28} - 3\sqrt{3})$

   Part B: $\dfrac{\sqrt{12}(2\sqrt{48})}{7\sqrt{3}}$

2. Perform the following operations and write the answers in radical form.
   Part A: $12^{\frac{1}{2}}\left(2^{\frac{1}{2}} + 3^{\frac{1}{2}}\right)\left(2^{\frac{1}{2}} - 3^{\frac{1}{2}}\right)$

   Part B: $\dfrac{12 \cdot 2^{\frac{1}{2}}}{27^{\frac{1}{3}}}$

3. Find the value of x if $9^{\frac{1}{2}} \cdot 9^{\frac{1}{2}} = \sqrt[x]{81}$.

4. Find the value of z if $z^{\frac{1}{2}} \cdot 16^{\frac{1}{4}} = \dfrac{2\sqrt{8} \cdot \sqrt{49}}{2\sqrt{2}}$.

5. Prove that $\sqrt{8} \cdot \sqrt{2} = 10 - 3 \cdot 4^{\frac{1}{2}}$.

6. What is the area of a rectangle that measures $3\sqrt{5} - 4\sqrt{12}$ by $\sqrt{125}$?

7. The area of a parallelogram is $8\sqrt{90}$ and the base is $2\sqrt{5}$. What is the height of the parallelogram?

Section 1 – Topic 7
Understanding Polynomial Expressions

1. Write $9x + 3x^2 - 4x^5 + x^3 + 2x^4$ in standard form.

2. Determine the type and degree of each of the following polynomial expressions.

    $9x^4y^9$

    $x^4 - 3x^2 + 7x^5$

    $19a^6b^2 + 8ab^3c - 27a^7$

3. Consider the following polynomial expression: $4x^5 - 16x^2 + 13x^8$.

    Part A: Write the polynomial expression in standard form.

    Part B: What is the degree of the polynomial?

    Part C: How many terms are in the polynomial?

    Part D: What is the leading term?

    Part E: What is the leading coefficient?

4. Match the polynomial in the left column with its descriptive feature in the right column.

    A. $x^3 + 3x^2 - 2x + 7$
    B. $3a^3b^6$
    C. $3x^4 - 9x^3 + 5x^8$
    D. $7a^3b^2 + 18ab^2c - 9a^3$
    E. $2x^5 - 9x^3 + 8x^7$
    F. $4x^8 - 7x^2 + 9$
    G. $x^2 - 7$

    I. 9th degree monomial
    II. Constant term of -7
    III. 7th degree polynomial
    IV. Leading coefficient of 4
    V. Four terms
    VI. 5th degree polynomial
    VII. Equivalent to $5x^8 + 3x^4 - 9x^3$

5. Write a binomial expression in standard form that has a degree of 4.

6. Write a trinomial expression in standard form that has a degree of 5.

7. Janae wrote the following polynomial expression: $2x^5 - 4x^3 + 6x^8$. Janae claimed it was a trinomial with a leading coefficient of 2. Justin argued back claiming that it was a trinomial with a leading coefficient of 6. Who is correct? Explain.

8. Ladarius wrote the following monomial expression: $5x^8y^3$. Ladarius said the monomial had a degree of 11. Ayla said the monomial had a degree of 8. Who is correct? Explain.

Practice Book - Section 1: Expressions

Section 1 – Topic 8
Operations with Polynomials – Part 1

1. Match each expression in the left column to its equivalent expression in the right column. Use the table below to write the letters that correspond to each of the numbers.

_____	$7(12)$	A. $5(1 + 3a)$
_____	$3(15)$	B. $3(a + 3)$
_____	$3a + 9$	C. $3(x + y + z)$
_____	$9a + 3$	D. $7(8 + 4)$
_____	$5 + 15a$	E. $3(x + 2y + 3z)$
_____	$10 + 5a$	F. $5(2 + a)$
_____	$3x + 6y + 9z$	G. $3(3a + 1)$
_____	$3x + 3y + 3z$	H. $(2 + 1)(15)$

2. Write an equivalent expression for $4(a + 5)$ by modeling and by using the distributive property.

3. Write an equivalent expression for $5(2x + y - 3z)$ by modeling and by using the distributive property.

4. The recommended heart rate for weight management exercise and improving cardio fitness, in beats per minute, depends on a person's age and can be represented by the expression $0.7(220 - a)$.

   Part A: What does the variable in the expression represent?

   Part B: Rewrite the expression using the distributive property.

   Part C: What is the recommended heart rate for a 20-year-old person?

5. Coach Smith is buying equipment for his soccer team. He has 11 players and each player needs three uniforms, two shin guards, one ball, and two pairs of cleats.

   Part A: Write an algebraic expression to represent this situation.

   Part B: If each uniform costs $48.00, each shin guard costs $5.00, each ball costs $17.00, and each pair of cleats costs $89.00, determine how much Coach Smith will spend, before taxes, on equipment for his soccer team.

6. Logan is building a game room adjacent to his living room so that both rooms will have the same width. He created a model on a piece of paper, shown below.

   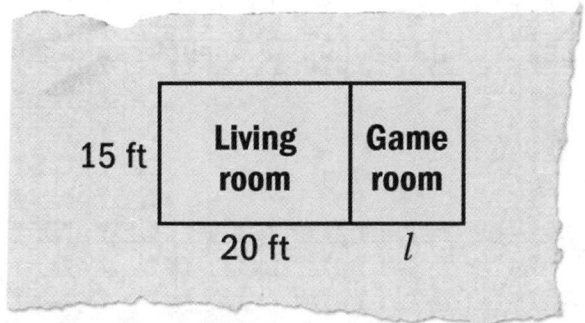

   Part A: Write an expression for the total area of both rooms by using the distributive property.

   Part B: If the length of the game room is 15 feet, what is the total square footage of the two rooms?

7. The state of Maine encourages recycling by giving refunds for certain recycled items. When you recycle a glass bottle, you get back $0.05, when you recycle an aluminum can, you get back $0.10, and when you recycle a plastic bottle, you get back $0.15.

   Part A: Drinks in a glass bottle cost $2.00, drinks in an aluminum can cost $0.50, and drinks in a plastic bottle cost $1.50. You plan to purchase two of each. Use the distributive property to write an expression that represents the amount of money you will spend.

   Part B: You plan to recycle all of the items you purchased. Use the distributive property to write an expression to represent the amount of refund you will receive.

   Part C: After receiving the refund, how much was your net cost for the items?
   Hint: Net cost is equal to the total cost minus the amount of your refund.

Practice Book - Section 1: Expressions

8. Suppose you are building a rectangular pen for your goats. You use 400 feet of fencing for the pen. Let l represent the pen's length (in feet).

   Part A: Which of the following expressions could represent the width of the pen?

   Ⓐ $2l + 400$
   Ⓑ $400 - 2l$
   Ⓒ $2l - 400$
   Ⓓ $400(2l)$

   Part B: Find the width of the pen if you make the pen 80 feet long.

   Part C: Find the width and the area of the pen if the length is 90 feet.

Section 1 – Topic 9
Operations with Polynomials – Part 2

1. Write an equivalent expression for $(x - 6)(x - 3)$ by using the distributive property and by modeling.

2. Write an equivalent expression for $(2m + 3)(m - 1)$.

3. Write an equivalent expression in standard form for $(5x - 4y)(7x^2 - 12x + 27)$.

4. Write an equivalent expression in standard form for $(6z - 3)(8z + 9) - 13(45 - 7z - z^2)$.

5. Write an equivalent expression for $(3m - 6)(8m^2 - 40m - 5)$.

6. Carlos is building a game room adjacent to his living room so that both rooms will have the same width. He created the model shown below.

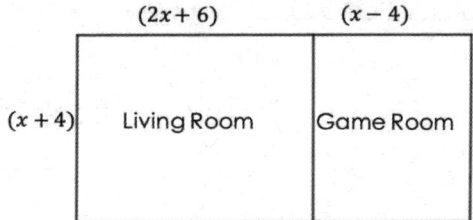

Part A: Write an expression for the total area of both rooms.

Part B: If the length of the game room is 12 feet, what is the total square footage of the two rooms?

Section 2: Equations and Inequalities
Student Learning Plan

Topic Number	Topic Name	Date Completed	Study Expert(s)	Check Your Understanding Score
1	Equations: True or False?			
2	Identifying Properties When Solving Equations			
3	Solving Equations			
4	Solving Equations Using the Zero Product Property			
5	Solving Inequalities – Part 1			
6	Solving Inequalities – Part 2			
7	Solving Compound Inequalities			
8	Rearranging Formulas			
9	Solution Sets to Equations with Two Variables			
Honors 1	Solving Power Equations			

Honors resources are available online.

What did you learn in this section? What questions do you still have?

Who was your favorite Study Expert for this section? Why?

18

Practice Book - Section 2: Equations and Inequalities

Section 2 – Topic 1
Equations: True or False?

1. Consider the statement: $4 - 3 + 5 = -6 + 8 + 4$. This is a mathematically correct sentence.

   Is the sentence true or false? Explain how you know.

2. Determine if the sentence is true. Select all that apply.

   ☐ $2 + 5 = 19 - 12$
   ☐ $\frac{4}{5} + \frac{1}{5} = 2 - 1 - 1$
   ☐ $5 - 4 - 3 - 2 - 1 = 30 - 34 - 1$
   ☐ $2(x + 8) = 2x - 8$
   ☐ $2(x + 5) - 4x = 3(x - 2) - 5x + 16$

3. Determine whether the following number sentences are TRUE or FALSE. Justify your answer.

   Part A: $7 + 5 + 3 + x = x + 3 + 12$

   Part B: $\frac{1}{2} - \frac{5}{8} - \frac{7}{9} = \frac{7}{9} - \frac{5}{8} - \frac{1}{2}$

   Part C: $6^3 + 5^2 = 18 + 5^2$

   Part D: $(2 + 2)^2 = 2^2 \cdot 2^2$

4. For the equation, $x - 7 = 24$, can a value be substituted for x to make the equation a true number sentence? How many values could be substituted for x and have a true number sentence?

5. Consider $x + 4 = x + 8$. What values could be substituted for x to make this a true number sentence? Explain how you know.

6. Determine what value(s) for the variable would make each algebraic equation a true number sentence.

   $m^2 = 81$ is true for _____.

   $6p = 3p + 2p + p$ is true for _____.

   $r + 74 = r - 74$ is true for _____.

7. Which of the following has the correct solution given for x? Check all that apply.

☐ $3x - 3 = 24; x = 9$

☐ $4 + x + 5 - x = 20; x = 3$

☐ $\frac{x+5}{7} = 5; x = 30$

☐ $9 = 2x - 3; x = 6$

☐ $50 = \frac{1}{3}x + 5; x = 48$

Section 2 – Topic 2
Identifying Properties When Solving Equations

1. The following pairs of equations are equivalent. Describe the operation that occurred in the second equation.

   Part A: $3 + 9 = 12$ and $3 + 9 - 5 = 12 - 5$

   Part B: $x - 4 = 7$ and $x - 4 + 4 = 7 + 4$

   Part C: $2(6) = 12$ and $\frac{2(6)}{2} = \frac{12}{2}$

   Part D: $\frac{x}{2} = 5$ and $2 \cdot \frac{x}{2} = 2 \cdot 5$

2. Complete the following table with the properties used to solve $4(x + 3) = 20$.

Statements	Proof
$4(x + 3) = 20$	Given
$4x + 12 = 20$	
$4x = 8$	
$x = 2$	

3. Complete the following table with the mathematical statements that correspond to the proofs used to solve $\frac{4(x-3)}{3} = 20$.

Statements	Proof
$\frac{4(x-3)}{3} = 20$	Given
	Multiplication Property of Equality
	Distributive Property
	Addition Property of Equality
	Division Property of Equality

4. Consider the equations $5x + 10 = 30$ and $5(x + 10) = 30$.

   Do they have the same solution? Why or why not?

5. Consider the equations $3x + 2 = 14$ and $2 + 3x = 14$.

   Do they have the same solution? Why or why not?

6. Consider the equation $3(x + 2) + 3x = 36$.

   Without solving, name all the properties that would be used to solve the equation.

7. Consider the equation $\frac{x}{3} + 7 = 13$.

   Part A: Write an equivalent equation using the multiplication property of equality.

   Part B: What properties will you use next to solve the equation?

8. Solve the following equation. Justify each step.

$$0.2x + 3.1 - 2.1x = 0.3(x - 5) + 0.2$$

9. Write an equation in which the distributive property, commutative property, associative property, addition or subtraction property of equality, and multiplication or division property of equality can be used to find the solution.

10. Solve the equation that you wrote in Question 9, justifying each step.

Practice Book - Section 2: Equations and Inequalities

Section 2 – Topic 3
Solving Equations

1. Solve each equation. For each step, identify the property used.

   Part A: $18 = 6(2x - 8)$

   Part B: $8 + 3b = -13$

   Part C: $\frac{x-3}{4} = 12$

   Part D: $14 + 3n = 8n - 3(n - 4)$

   Part E: $22x + 11 = 4x - 7$

2. During summer vacation, you charge people $8 per hour for swimming lessons and a $20 registration fee. If you make $52 one day, how many hours did you spend teaching lessons?

3. Lacoste Middle School surveyed its student population about their favorite mobile apps. The 786 students who listed Facebook as their favorite app represented 32 fewer students than two times the number of students who listed Instagram as their favorite app. How many students listed Instagram as their favorite app?

4. The 2015 senior class from Puma High School raised funds for an end-of-the-year party at Club Sizzle. It costs $4,000 to rent out Club Sizzle plus $20 per student for food and drinks. If the senior class raised $11,000, how many students can attend the end of year party?

5. Alex sells cars at Keith Palmer Ford. He earns $400 a week plus $150 per car he sells. If he earned $1450 last week, how many cars did he sell?

Practice Book - Section 2: Equations and Inequalities

Section 2- Topic 4
Solving Equations Using the Zero Product Property

1. Solve the following equation using the zero product property.

   $(x + 8)(x + 11) = 0$

2. Solve the following equation using the zero product property.

   $(x + 9)(4x - 1) = 0$

3. Solve the following equation using the zero product property.

   $5(-v - 5) \cdot 3(v - 8) = 0$

4. Manny was given the equation $(x + 2)(x - 17) = 0$ and asked to find the zeros. The solutions he came up with were $x = 2$ and $x = -17$.

   Are his solutions correct? Justify your answer.

5. Which equations have the same pair of solutions? Select all that apply.

   ☐ $(x + 6)(x - 6) = 0$
   ☐ $(x + 6)(x + 6) = 0$
   ☐ $(x - 6)(x - 6) = 0$
   ☐ $(2x + 12)(2x - 12) = 0$
   ☐ $(2x - 12)(x - 12) = 0$
   ☐ $(x + 12)(x - 12) = 0$
   ☐ $(x + 12)(x - 6) = 0$

6. Ted and Maggie solved the following equation, $(3x - 2)(x + 5) = 0$. Their work is shown below.

Ted	Maggie
$(3x - 2)(x + 5) = 0$	$(3x - 2)(x + 5) = 0$
$3x - 2 = 0$ or $x + 5 = 0$	$3x - 2 = 0$ or $x + 5 = 0$
$3x = 2$ or $x = -5$	$3x = -2$ or $x = 5$
$x = \frac{2}{3}$ or $x = -5$	$x = -\frac{2}{3}$ or $x = 5$

   Who is correct? Correct the mistake in the incorrect work.

Practice Book - Section 2: Equations and Inequalities

Section 2 – Topic 5
Solving Inequalities – Part 1

1. Match the inequalities below with one of the statements in the table. Not all inequalities will be used.

$x \leq 35$	$x \leq 12$	$x > 3$
$x \leq 10$	$x > 32$	$x \geq 10$
$x \leq 5$	$x \geq 35$	$x \geq 3$
$x \geq 32$	$x \geq 12$	$x < 10$
$x < 40$	$x \leq 40$	$x \geq 5$

Statement	Inequality
A student will study German for at least 3 years.	
All employees work less than 40 hours.	
There are at least 35 people in the emergency room.	
The carton holds at most 12 eggs.	
There are no more than 10 gallons of gas in the tank.	
There are fewer than 10 yards of fabric left.	
The temperature is above 32°F.	
Years of experience cannot be less than 5 years.	

2. Consider the diagrams below.

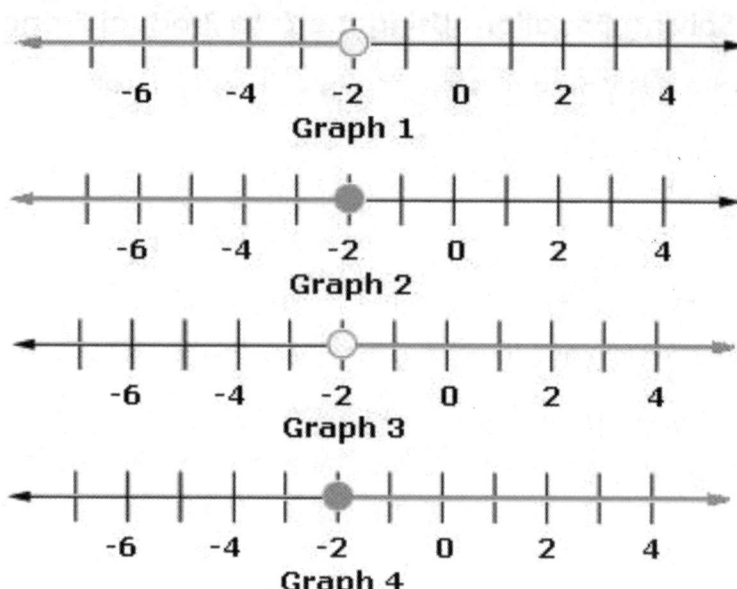

Write the inequality for each graph shown above:

Graph 1:   Graph 2:

Graph 3:   Graph 4:

3. The Latino Rams at Englewood High School are seeking to raise at least $750 in a fundraiser to pay for their end-of-the year field trip to Islands of Adventures.

   Part A: Write an inequality to represent this situation.

   x ≥ 750

   Part B: Graph the inequality on a number line.

   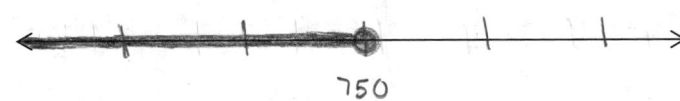
   750

4. Find the solution set to each inequality. Express the solution in set notation.

   Part A: $6m + 2 < 5m - 4$

   −5m   −5m
   m + 2 < −4
   −2   −2
   m < −6   {m | m < −6}

   Part B: $\frac{a}{5} + 8 \leq 13$

   −8 −8
   $\frac{5}{1} \cdot \frac{a}{5} \leq 5 \times 5$
   a ≤ 25   {a | a ≤ 25}

   Part C: $-3(x - 7) > -27$

   −3x + 21 > −27   {x | x > 16}
   −21   −21
   $\frac{-3x}{-3} > \frac{-48}{-3}$
   x > 16

   Part D: $8(p - 6) > 4(p - 4)$

   8p − 48 > 4p − 16
   8p − 4p > 48 − 16   {p | p > 8}
   $\frac{4p}{4} > \frac{32}{4}$
   p > 8

Section 2 – Topic 6
Solving Inequalities – Part 2

1. In order for Brady to earn a B in his biology course, his test scores must average at least 80%. On the first 5 tests, he has an average of 77%. There is one test remaining in the course. What is the minimum score Brady needs to earn on the last test to receive a B in the class?

   6. $\frac{5 \cdot 77 + x}{6} \geq 80 \cdot 6$ $\frac{385 + x \geq 480}{-385 \quad -385}$

   5·77 + x ≥ 480   x ≥ 95

   385 + x ≥ 480   {x | x ≥ 95}

2. Shawn has been hired as a sales associate at the Horizon Mobile Phone Company. He has two salary options. He can either receive a fixed salary of $750.00 per week or a salary of $400.00 per week plus an 8% commission of his weekly sales. Which solution set among the options below represents the dollar amount of sales that he must generate each week in order for the option with commission to be the better choice?

   Ⓐ {s|s > $810.00}
   Ⓑ {s|s > $1150.00}
   Ⓒ {s|s > $4,375.00}
   Ⓓ {s|s > $9,375.00}

3. In GeoTown, there are 210 teenagers that own a tablet. This is at least $\frac{4}{5}$ of all teenagers that live in GeoTown. What is the maximum number of teenagers who live in GeoTown?

4. Ms. Ache is paid $1,250 per week but is fined $100 each day she is late to work. Ms. Ache wants to make at least $3,000 over the next three weeks so she can take a vacation.

   Over the next three weeks, what is the maximum number of days she can be late to work and still reach her goal of making at least $3,000?

5. The Hot Summer Fair is coming to town! Admission to the fair costs $12.99 and each ride costs $1.75. You have $35 to spend at the fair including admission.

   Part A: Write an inequality that represents this situation.

   Part B: Solve the inequality to determine the maximum number of rides you can enjoy at the Hot Summer Fair.

Section 2 – Topic 7
Solving Compound Inequalities

1. Match the compound inequalities below with one of the statements in the table. Not all inequalities will be used.

$-42 < x < 102$	$20 \leq x < 32$	$x > 0$ and $x \leq 10$
$x < 25$ or $x \geq 62$	$16 \leq x \leq 20$	$x < 54$ and $x \geq 72$
$x < 54$ or $x \geq 72$	$x > 0$ and $x < 6$	$x > 85$ or $x < 65$
$16 < x < 20$	$25 < x \leq 62$	$x > 85$ and $x < 65$
$x \geq 20$ or $x < 32$	$-42 \leq x \leq 102$	$x > 0$ or $x < 6$

All real numbers that are less than six but more than 0.	
All real numbers between −42 and 102, inclusive.	
All positive real numbers less than or equal to ten.	
All students earning above an 85 or below a 65 were asked to report to the media center for further instructions.	
The expected weight must be greater than or equal to 20 pounds but less than 32 pounds.	
Students under 25 or seniors at or above 62 get a discount.	
If the temperature is at or above 72°F or below 54°F, the samples in the biology lab are no longer useful.	
Cookies must be baked between 16 and 20 minutes.	

Practice Book - Section 2: Equations and Inequalities

2. Graph $x \leq 8$ and $x > -1$.

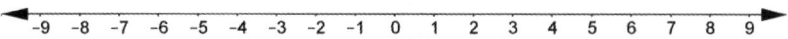

3. Graph $x < -6$ or $x \geq 4$.

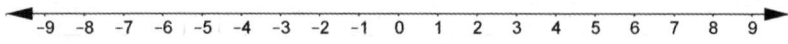

4. Write a compound inequality for the following graphs.

   Part A:

   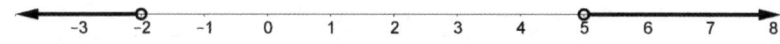

   Part B:

   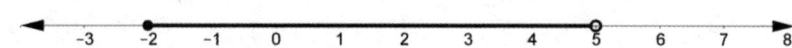

5. Amaya's test scores in Algebra 1 are 78 and 91. She has one more test left and wants to earn a B for the course, which is from 80-89 inclusive.

   Part A: Write a compound inequality to represent the situation.

   Part B: Solve the inequality to find the range of scores Amaya has to earn to get a B in Algebra 1.

6. Uncle Sammy invests money on stocks and makes 7 to 13 percent of the invested money.

   Calculate the range of money Sammy will make if he invests his next paycheck of $2,300.

7. Solve and graph the following compound inequalities.

   Part A: $7 \leq 5x + 2 < 22$

   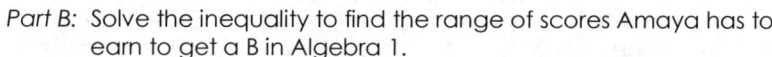

   Part B: $-4p \geq 12$ or $8 - 2p < 12$

   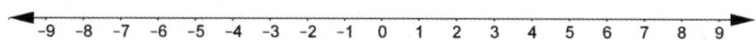

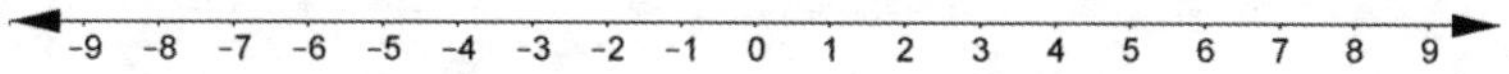

Practice Book - Section 2: Equations and Inequalities

8. An Indy car driver has to be a certain height to fit into the racecar. Consider the inequality $175 \leq 3x - 17 \leq 187$, where x represents the height of the driver in inches.

   What is the range for the height of an Indy car driver?

9. Peyton is altering her new jacket to enter it into the Bodacious Bedazzling Contest. In order for a garment to be considered "bedazzled", it must contain a number of gems that fall within the range of the following inequality $132 \leq \frac{1}{2}x + 7 \leq 193$.

   Find the range of gems Peyton must use to enter her jacket into the contest.

Section 2 – Topic 8
Rearranging Formulas

1. Consider the following equation, $bh + hr = 25$.

   Part A: Solve the equation for h.

   Part B: Solve the equation for r.

2. Consider the following equation $x = \frac{r-h}{y}$.

   Part A: Solve the equation for h.

   Part B: Solve the equation for r.

3. Charlize and Camille solved the equation $4x - 2y = 8$ for y. Their work is shown below.

Charlize	Camille
$4x - 2y = 8$	$4x - 2y = 8$
$-2y = 8 + 4x$	$-2y = 8 - 4x$
$y = -4 - 2x$	$y = -4 + 2x$

Which student solved the equation correctly? Justify your answer.

4. Solve the following equation for p.

   $2m = \frac{p-q}{r}$

5. The formula to find the volume of a sphere is $V = \frac{4}{3}\pi r^3$, where r is the radius of the sphere. What is the formula in terms of r?

Section 2 – Topic 9
Solution Sets to Equations with Two Variables

1. Martha can complete 15 activities a day at summer camp. She can choose between crafts or sports.

   Part A: Define two variables and create an equation to represent the situation.

   Variable 1:

   Variable 2:

   Equation:

   Part B: What are three possible combinations of crafts and sports that Martha can do?

   Part C: Create a graph that represents the solutions to the equation from Part A.

   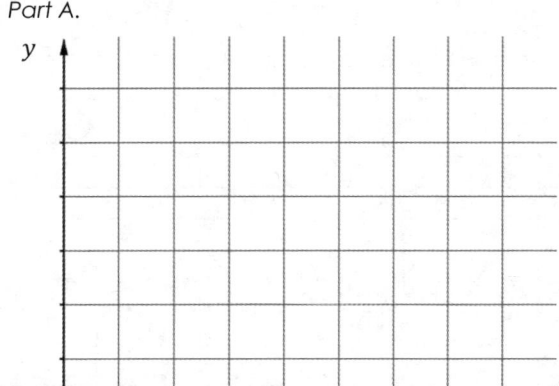

Part D: Are the solutions to the graph discrete or continuous? Explain your answer.

2. Mahagony's favorite brand of ice cream is Ben & Jerry's. This weekend while she was doing her grocery shopping, she bought 9 single-serving containers, some "That's My Jam", and some "Cherry Garcia".

   Part A: Define two variables and create an equation to represent the situation.

   Variable 1:

   Variable 2:

   Equation:

   Part B: What are three possible combinations of "That's My Jam" and "Cherry Garcia" containers Mahagony might have purchased?

   Part C: Create a graph that represents the solutions to the equation from Part A.

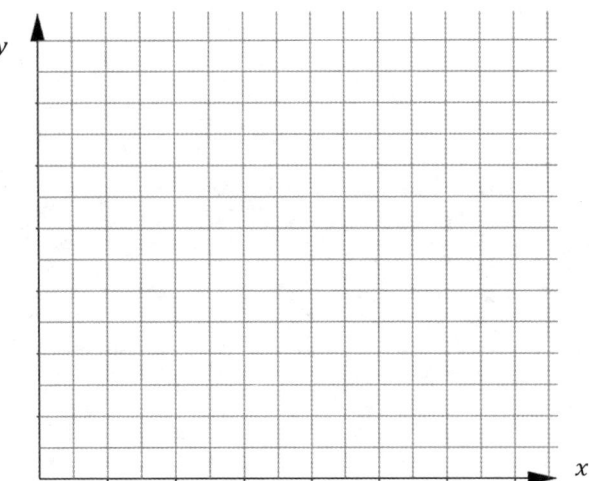

Part D: Are the solutions to the graph discrete or continuous? Explain your answer.

3. The sum of two numbers is 23.

   Part A: Define two variables and create an equation to represent the situation.

   Variable 1:

   Variable 2:

   Equation:

   Part B: What are three possible combinations of numbers that will satisfy the situation?

   Part C: Create a graph that represents the solutions to the equation from Part A.

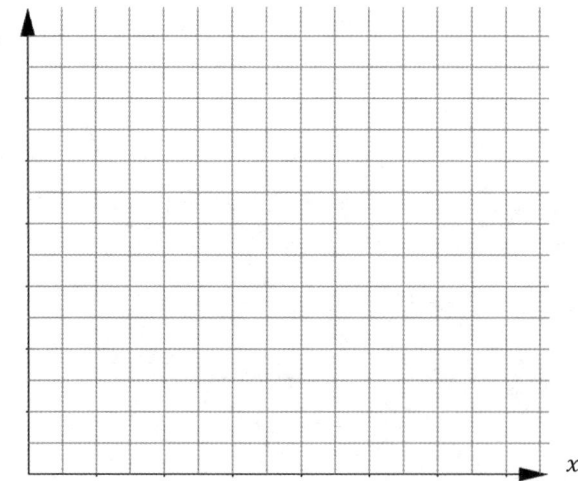

30

Practice Book - Section 2: Equations and Inequalities

Part D: Are the solutions to the graph discrete or continuous? Explain your answer.

4. Demarcus' workout playlist consists of classic rock songs and rap songs. His playlist contains a total of 47 songs.

   Which of the following statements represent the number of classic rock and rap songs on Demarcus' playlist? Select all that apply.

   ☐ $x + y = 47$
   ☐ 24 and 24
   ☐ 43 and 4
   ☐ $x = y + 47$
   ☐ $y = -x + 47$
   ☐ 13 and 34

5. Debahni is moving boxes into her new house. She is able to move 17 boxes per hour. She is only able to move the small and medium size boxes.

   Part A: Define two variables and create an equation to represent the situation.

   Variable 1:

   Variable 2:

   Equation:

Part B: What are three possible combinations of numbers that will satisfy the situation?

Part C: Is this an example of a discrete or continuous function?

6. Mr. Mayntz's math class is made up of 29 students. Some of the students are male and some are female.

   Which of the following statements represent the number of males and females in Mr. Mayntz's class? Select all that apply.

   ☐ 23.5 males and 5.5 females
   ☐ $x + y = 29$
   ☐ 12 males and 17 females
   ☐ $x = y - 29$
   ☐ $y = -x - 29$

Practice Book - Section 2: Equations and Inequalities

Section 3: Introduction to Functions
Student Learning Plan

Topic Number	Topic Name	Date Completed	Study Expert(s)	Check Your Understanding Score
1	What is a Function?			
2	Representing, Naming, and Evaluating Functions			
3	Adding and Subtracting Functions			
4	Multiplying Functions			
5	Closure Property			
6	Real-World Combinations and Compositions of Functions			
7	Key Features of Graphs of Functions – Part 1			
8	Key Features of Graphs of Functions – Part 2			
9	Average Rate of Change Over an Interval			
10	Transformations of Functions			
Honors 1	Rewriting Rational Expressions and the Remainder Theorem			

*Honors resources are available online.

What did you learn in this section? What questions do you still have?

Who was your favorite Study Expert for this section? Why?

Practice Book - Section 3: Introduction to Functions

Section 3 – Topic 1
What is a Function?

1. A group of students were discussing whether the relationship on the graph is a function.

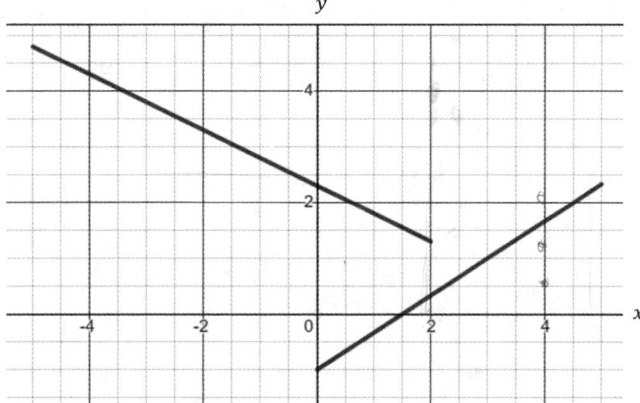

Ed: The relationship is not a function because if I draw a horizontal line at $y = 2$, the horizonal line crosses the graph at two points.

Debra: The relationship is a function because it is a graph of two different lines.

Alejandro: The relationship is not a function because $x = 1$ has two different y-values.

Antoine: The relationship is a function because I can write an equation for a line.

Which students are **not** correct and what is the flaw in their argument?

Ed is wrong because he is supposed to draw a Verticle line to check, not a horizantal line.

Debra is wrong because the relationship on the graph is not a function, and a function can have two different lines.

Antoine is wrong because the relationship on the graph is not a funcion, and you can still write an equation for a non-function.

Therefore, Alejandro is Correct

2. Complete the sentence about the two given relations.

Relation A: $\{(-8, -6), (-8, -7), (-8, -6), (-8, -5)\}$

Relation B:

x	y
3.78	3.78
-3.78	3.78
23.7	23.7
0	0
-12.43	12.43

Because ○ Relation A ● Relation B , ○ can be written using $f(x)$, ● has one-to-one correspondence, it is a function.

3. Consider the following incomplete mapping diagrams.

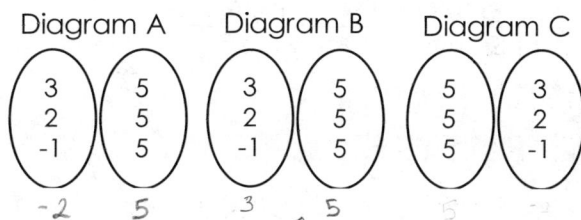

Part A: Complete Diagram A so that it is a function.

Part B: Is it possible to complete Diagram B so that it is NOT a function? If so, complete the diagram to show a relation, but not a function. If not, justify your reasoning.

Part C: Is it possible to complete the mapping diagram for Diagram C so it represents a function? If so, complete the diagram to show a function. If not, justify your reasoning.

No, becaus it would be a verticle line.

4. The cost to manufacture x chairs can be represented by the function $C(x) = 36x$. Circle the pair of numbers (one in each box) that correctly completes the statement about the function.

If $C(63) = 2268$, then [0 / 6 / 63 / 378] chairs cost $ [6 / 189 / 378 / 2,268].

5. Which of the following relations are not functions? Select all that apply.

☐ $\{(1,3),(3,7),(5,11),(7,15),(9,19)\}$
☐ $\{(1,3),(1,7),(5,11),(5,15),(9,19)\}$
☐ $\{(-2,4),(-1,1),(0,0),(1,1),(2,4)\}$
☐ $\{(2,4),(1,1),(0,0),(1,-1),(2,-4)\}$
☐ $\{(6,3),(4,1),(2,1),(0,-1),(-2,-3)\}$
☐ $\{(1,3),(3,7),(3,11),(7,15),(9,19)\}$
☐ $\{(1,3),(3,7),(5,11),(9,15),(9,19)\}$

Section 3 – Topic 2
Representing, Naming, and Evaluating Functions

1. A ball is thrown into the air with an initial velocity of 22 meters per second. The quadratic function $h(t) = -4.9t^2 + 22t + 5.5$ represents the height of the ball above the ground, in meters, with respect to time t, in seconds.

Part A: Determine $h(3)$ and explain what it represents.

The graph below represents the height of the ball with respect to time.

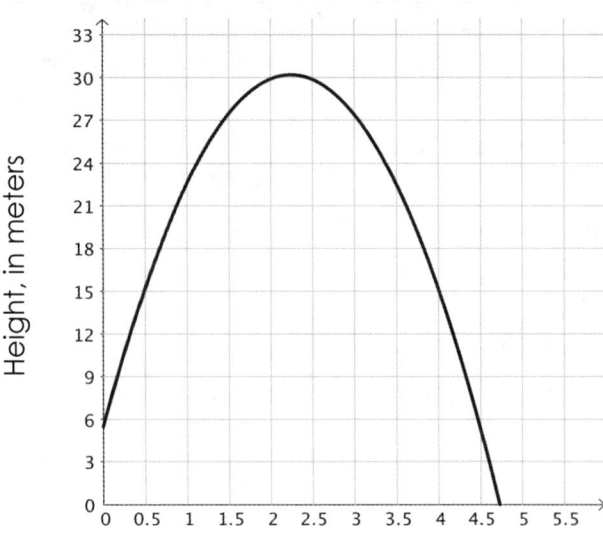

Height of the Ball Over Time

Part B: What is a reasonable domain for the function?

Part C: What is a reasonable range for the function?

34

Practice Book - Section 3: Introduction to Functions

2. On the moon, the time, in seconds, it takes for an object to fall a distance, d, in feet, is given by the function $f(d) = 1.11\sqrt{d}$.

   Part A: Determine $f(2)$ and explain what it represents.

   Part B: The Imbrium Basin is the largest basin on the moon. A reasonable domain for the height above the lowest point in the basin is given by $\{d | 0 \leq d \leq 3805774\}$. What does this tell you about the basin?

   Part C: How long would it take a rock to drop from the rim to the bottom of the basin?

3. The function that represents the amount of caffeine, in milligrams, remaining in a body after drinking two Mountain Dew sodas is given by $f(t) = 110(0.8855)^t$ where t is time in hours. How much caffeine is left in a person's body 18 hours after drinking two Mountain Dew sodas?

4. The function $f(t) = |98.6 - x|$, represents a person's variance from normal body temperature, where x represents a person's current body temperature in degrees Fahrenheit. Medical professionals say healthy individuals should have a variance of no more than 0.5°F.

   Part A: What can be said of an individual with a body temperature of 99.4°F? Justify your answer.

   Part B: What can be said of an individual with a body temperature of 98.4°F? Justify your answer.

   Part C: What is a reasonable domain that would indicate the individual is not healthy?

Section 3 – Topic 3
Adding and Subtracting Functions

1. Let $f(x) = 7x^2 - 5x + 3$ and $g(x) = 2x^2 + 4x - 6$.

   Part A: Find $f(x) + g(x)$

   Part B: Find $f(x) - g(x)$

   Part C: Find $g(x) - f(x)$

2. The perimeter of the triangle below is $4x + 3y$. Find the measure of the missing side.

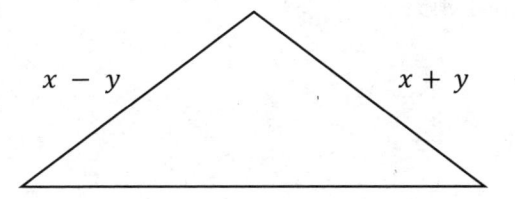

   (triangle with sides $x - y$ and $x + y$)

Practice Book - Section 3: Introduction to Functions

3. The perimeter of a trapezoid is $39a - 7$. Three sides have the following lengths: $9a$, $5a + 1$, and $17a - 6$.

   What is the length of the fourth side?

4. Jocelyn and Lorlesha are comparing the size of their villages in the Clash of Clans app. The area of Jocelyn's village is represented by the polynomial, $2w^2 + 10w + 12$. The area of Lorlesha's village is represented by the polynomial, $3w^2 + 4w - 5$, where w represents the width, in meters of their Town Hall.

   Part A: Find the expression that represents the additional area of Jocelyn's village.

   Part B: Find the expressions that represents the combined total area of their villages.

Section 3 – Topic 4
Multiplying Functions

1. Evaluate $g(p) \cdot h(p)$ by modeling or by using the distributive property.

   $g(p) = (p - 2)$ and $h(p) = (p^3 + 4p^2 - 2)$

2. Evaluate $f(x) \cdot g(x)$ by modeling or by using the distributive property.

   $f(x) = (-3x + 2)$ and $g(x) = (2x^2 - 5x - 1)$

3. Jamie used the distributive property to find the product of $s(t)$ and $h(t)$. His work was marked incorrect. Identify Jamie's mistake. What advice would you give Jamie to avoid this mistake in the future?

   $s(t) \cdot h(t) = (3x - 4)(2x - 8)$
   $= 6x^2 - 24x - 8x - 32$
   $= 6x^2 - 32x - 32$

4. The figure below shows the penalty box and the goal box of a soccer field. The penalty box is the larger rectangle.

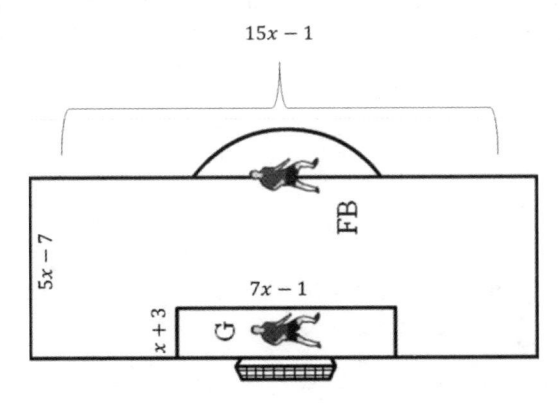

Penalty box dimensions: $15x - 1$ by $5x - 7$
Goal box dimensions: $7x - 1$ by $x + 3$

Part A: Find the area of the penalty box.

Part B: Find the area of the goal box.

Part C: Find the area of the penalty box not covered by the goal box.

Section 3 – Topic 5
Closure Property

1. For the following exercises determine if the closure property applies to the following statements by circling 'True' or 'False'. Then provide an example of each statement.

Statement A	Answer Choice	
Polynomials are closed under addition.	True	False
Example:		

Statement B	Answer Choice	
Polynomials are closed under subtraction.	True	False
Example:		

Statement C	Answer Choice	
Polynomials are closed under multiplication.	True	False
Example:		

Statement D	Answer Choice	
Polynomials are closed under division.	True	False
Example:		

Practice Book - Section 3: Introduction to Functions

2. Check the boxes for the following sets that are closed under the given operations.

Set	+	-	×	÷
{... −7, −6, −5, −4, −3}	☐	☐	☐	☐
{0, $\sqrt{1}$, $\sqrt{4}$, $\sqrt{9}$, $\sqrt{16}$, $\sqrt{25}$...}	☐	☐	☐	☐
{... $-\frac{10}{2}$, $-\frac{8}{2}$, $-\frac{6}{2}$, $-\frac{4}{2}$, $-\frac{2}{2}$...}	☐	☐	☐	☐

3. Consider the following polynomials.

$$ab^2 + 3ab + 8a^2$$
$$-5ab^2$$

Use the two polynomials to illustrate the following:

Part A: Polynomials are closed under addition.

Part B: Polynomials are closed under subtraction.

Part C: Polynomials are closed under multiplication.

Part D: Polynomials are not closed under division.

4. Ms. Adams claims that the closure properties for polynomials are closed when dividing polynomials. Mr. Aroxa claims that the closure properties for polynomials are not closed when dividing polynomials. Who is correct? Explain your answer.

Section 3 – Topic 6
Real-World Combinations and Compositions of Functions

1. The student government association is selling roses for Valentine's Day to raise money for their trip to the state convention. The cost of each rose is $1.50 and the florist charges a delivery fee of $25. The class plans to sell the roses for $5.00 each.

   Part A: Define the variable.

   Part B: Write a cost function.

   Part C: Write a revenue function.

   Part D: Write a profit function.

2. A local civic group is selling t-shirts to raise funds for Relay to Life. They plan to sell 2500 t-shirts for $10. They consider raising the t-shirt price in order to earn more profit. For each $1 increase, they will sell 100 fewer t-shirts. Let x represent the number of $1 increases.

   Part A: Write a function, $C(x)$, to represent the cost of one t-shirt based on the number of increases.

   Part B: Write a function, $T(x)$, to represent the number of t-shirts sold based on the number of increases.

   Part C: Write a revenue function, $R(x)$, for the t-shirt sale that could be used to maximize revenue.

3. Anna gets paid $8.75/hour working as a barista at Coffee Break. Her boss pays her $9.00/hour for creating the weekly advertisement signs. She works a total of 25 hours each week.

   Part A: Let x represent the hours that Anna works each week as a barista. Write a function, $h(x)$, to represent the amount of money that Anna earns working as a barista.

   Part B: Write a function, $f(x)$, to represent the hours Anna works creating the signs.

   Part C: Let s represent the number of hours that Anna works creating the signs. Create a function, $g(s)$, to represent the money Anna earns creating the signs.

   Part D: Find $g(f(x))$. What does this composite function represent?

   Part E: What functions could be combined to represent Anna's total earnings? Combine the functions to write an expression that can be used to represent Anna's total earnings, where x represents the number of hours she works as a barista.

Practice Book - Section 3: Introduction to Functions

4. Consider the following standards.

   MAFS.912.F-BF.1.1b: *Combine standard function types using arithmetic operation. For example, build a function that models the temperature of a cooling body by adding a constant function to a decaying exponential, and relate these functions to the model.*

   MAFS.912.F-BF.1.1c: *Compose functions. For example, if T(y) is the temperature in the atmosphere as a function of height, and h(t) is the height of a weather balloon as a function of time, then T(h(t)) is the temperature at the location of the weather balloon as a function of time.*

   Part A: Describe the difference in combining functions and composing functions.

   Part B: Give a real-world example of combining functions.

   Part C: Give a real-world example of composing functions.

Section 3 – Topic 7
Key Features of Graphs of Functions – Part 1

1. The following statement is false. Highlight the two words that should be interchanged to make it a true statement.

   In a function, every output value corresponds to exactly one input value.

2. The following graph fails the vertical line test and is not a function.

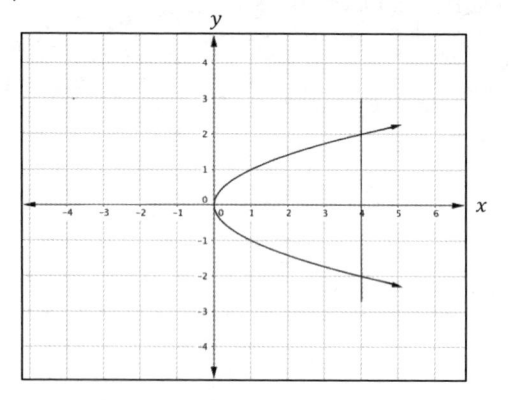

   Part A: Explain how the vertical line test shows that this relation is NOT a function.

   Part B: Name two points on the graph that show that this relation is NOT a function.

40

Practice Book - Section 3: Introduction to Functions

3. Sketch the graph of a relation that is a function.

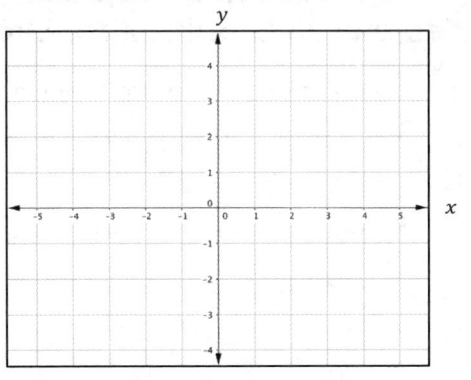

4. Sketch the graph of a relation that is NOT a function.

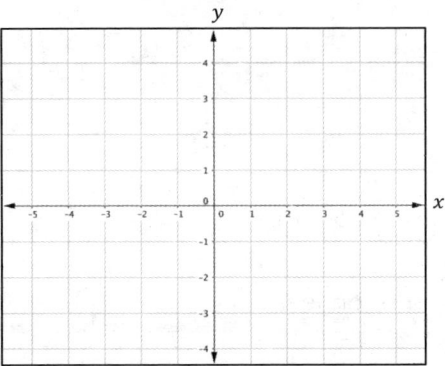

5. Consider the following scenarios. Determine if each one represents a function or not. Explain your answer.

   Part A: A golf ball is hit down a fairway. The golfer relates the time passed to the height of the ball.

   Part B: A trainer takes a survey of all the athletes in a school about their height, rounded to the nearest inch, and their grade level. The trainer relates their grade levels to their heights.

6. Use the word bank to complete the sentences below.

   | x–coordinate | y–coordinate | x–intercept | y–intercept | solution |

   a. The _____ of a graph is the location where the graph crosses the x–axis.
   b. The _____ of a graph is the location where the graph crosses the y–axis.
   c. The _____ of the y–intercept is always zero.
   d. The _____ of the x–intercept is always zero.
   e. The x–intercept is the _____ to a function or group.

7. The graph below represents a rock climber's height as she ascends a hill.

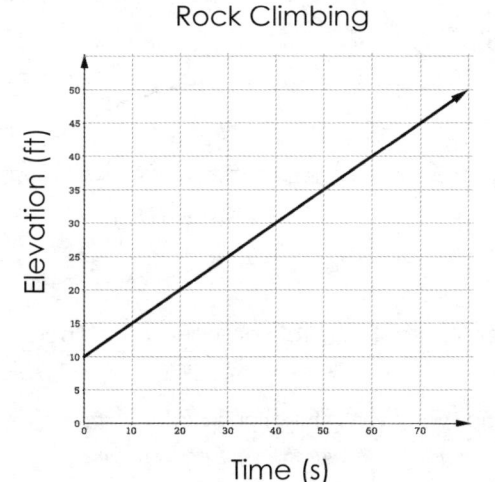

   Rock Climbing

   Part A: The above graph is (circle one) linear/nonlinear.

   Part B: Is the above graph a function? Explain.

Practice Book - Section 3: Introduction to Functions

Part C: What is the y-intercept and what does the y-intercept represent?

Part D: Why would there not be an x-intercept for this situation?

8. The graph below represents the path of a golf ball.

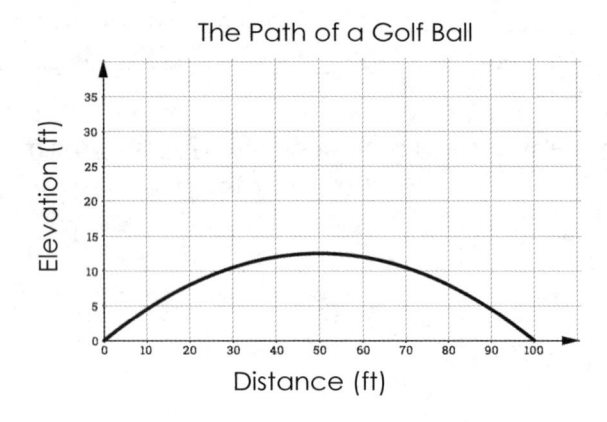

The Path of a Golf Ball

Part A: The above graph is (circle one) linear/nonlinear.

Part B: Is the above graph a function? Explain.

Part C: What is the y-intercept and what does the y-intercept represent?

Part D: What is the solution to this graph and what does it represent in this situation?

Section 3 – Topic 8
Key Features of Graphs of Functions – Part 2

1. Consider the following graph of an absolute value function.

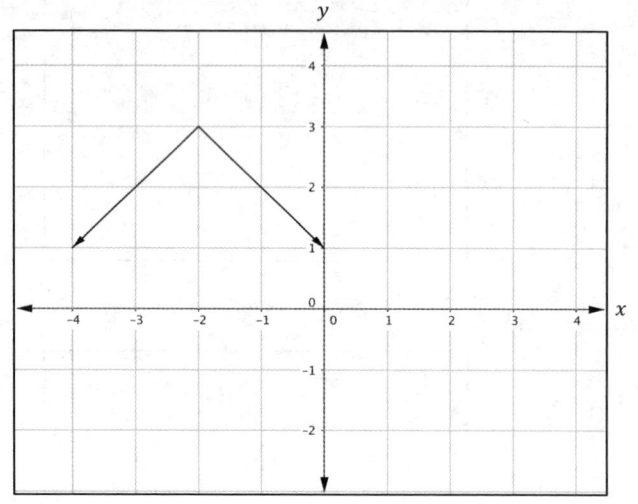

Part A: Define the domain.

Part B: Define the range.

Part C: Where is the graph increasing?

Part D: Where is the graph decreasing?

Part E: Identify any relative maximums.

Part F: Identify any relative minimums.

2. Consider the following graph of a quadratic function.

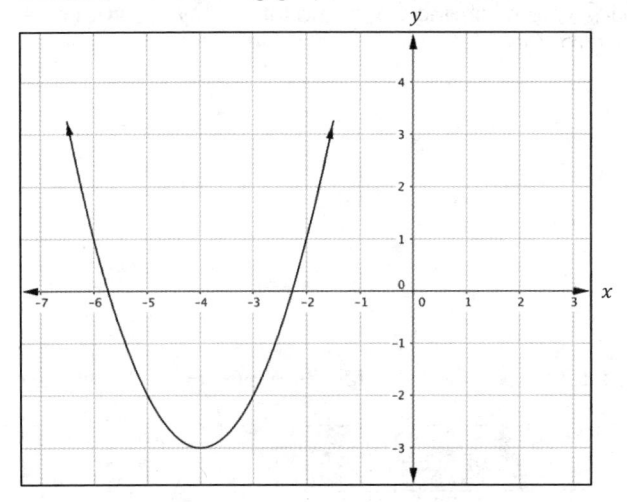

Part A: Define the domain.

Part B: Define the range.

Part C: Where is the graph increasing?

Part D: Where is the graph decreasing?

Part E: Identify any relative maximums.

Part F: Identify any relative minimums.

3. Consider the following graph of an exponential function.

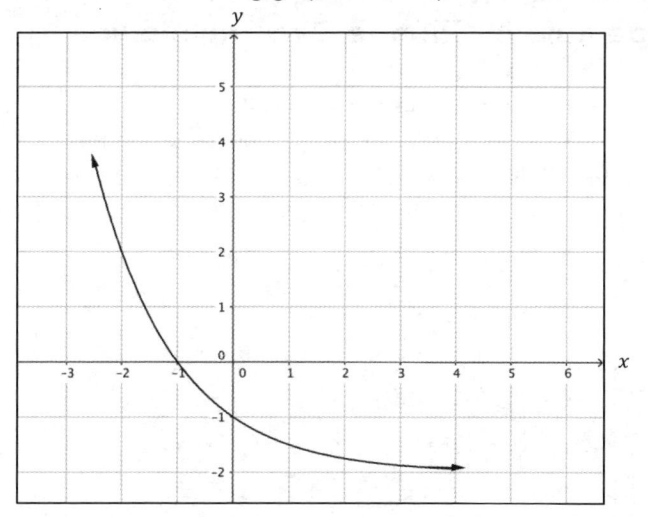

Part A: Define the domain.

Part B: Define the range.

Part C: Where is the graph increasing?

Part D: Where is the graph decreasing?

Part E: Identify any relative maximums.

Part F: Identify any relative minimums.

Practice Book - Section 3: Introduction to Functions

Section 3 – Topic 9
Average Rate of Change Over an Interval

1. Suppose that the cost of producing x tablets is defined by $c(x) = 200 + 10x + 0.2x^2$, where x represents the number of tablets produced. The graph below represents the function.

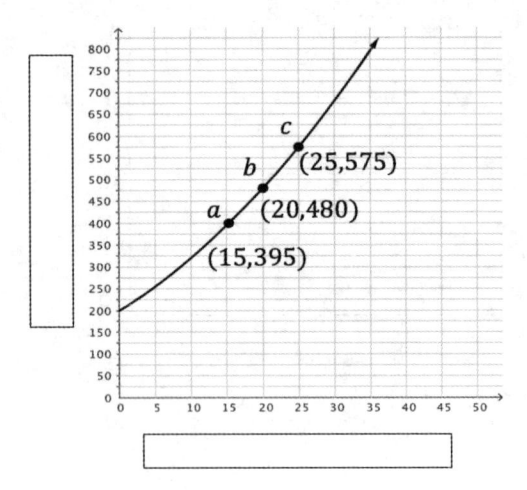

[Graph showing points a (15, 395), b (20, 480), c (25, 575)]

Part A: Complete the boxes to label the graph.

Part B: Find the average rate of change over the interval $[a, b]$.

Part C: Find the average rate of change over the interval $[b, c]$.

Part D: Compare the average rate of change over the interval $[a, b]$ with the average rate of change over the interval $[b, c]$. What does this represent in real life?

2. Consider the table for the exponential function, $p(x) = 2^x$, shown below.

Point	x	$p(x)$
A	0	1
B	2	4
C	4	16
D	6	64

Part A: Which of the following intervals would you expect to have the greatest rate of change? Explain your reasoning.

- ○ $[A, B]$
- ○ $[B, C]$
- ○ $[C, D]$

Part B: Find the rate of change of the three intervals to determine if your hypothesis in *Part A* was correct.

3. Consider the following graph of a quadratic function.

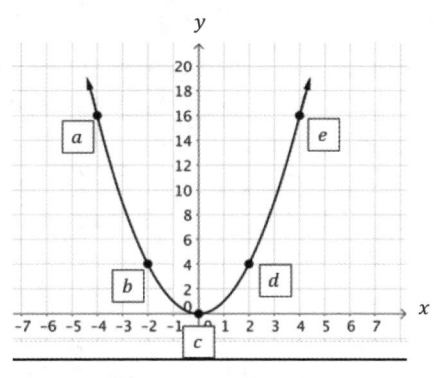

Part A: How can you quickly determine the intervals with the greatest rate of change by making observations from the graph?

Part B: Which intervals have the greatest rate of change?

Part C: Which intervals have the least rate of change?

Part D: Name two intervals that have equal rates of change.

4. Bradford hopped into his Ford Mustang GT to rush to Diana and tell her how fantastic his students did on the End of Course exam. His Mustang can go from 0 to 60 mph in a brief 4.7 seconds. Bradford accelerated to top speed quickly and then maintained a speed of 60 mph until he arrived at Diane's office.

Part A: Sketch the graph of the situation on the coordinate plane.

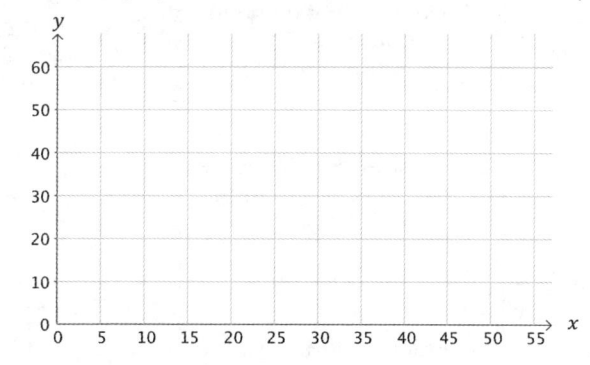

Part B: Over which interval would you have the greatest rate of change? Justify your answer.

Part C: What part of the situation represents the time when the graph has no rate of change?

Practice Book - Section 3: Introduction to Functions

Section 3 – Topic 10
Transformations of Functions

1. Label the following as transformations on the independent variable or the dependent variable and describe the transformation.

Function	Is the transformation on the independent or dependent variable?	Description of the transformation
↓ $f(x) + 3$	○ Independent Variable ⊗ Dependent Variable	up 3
↓ $f(x) - 3$	○ Independent Variable ⊗ Dependent Variable	down 3
$f(x + 3)$	⊗ Independent Variable ○ Dependent Variable	left 3
$f(x - 3)$	⊗ Independent Variable ○ Dependent Variable	right 3

2. The following table represents the function $h(x)$. Complete the table for $g(x)$, given $g(x) = \frac{1}{2}h(x)$.

x	$h(x)$
-4	256
-2	16
0	0
3	81
6	1296

x	$g(x)$
-4	128
-2	8
0	0
3	40.5
6	648

3. The following graph represents the function $f(x)$. Sketch and label the following functions on the same coordinate plane.

a. $f(x + 2)$

b. $f(x - 5)$

c. $f(x) + 2$

d. $f(x) - 5$

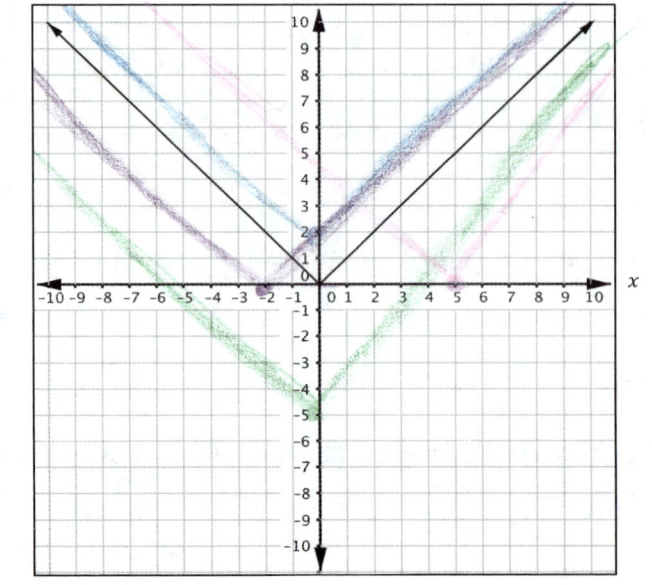

4. The following table represents the function $h(x)$. Complete the table for $g(x)$, given $g(x) = h\left(\frac{1}{4}x\right)$. The first two have been done for you!

x	$h(x)$
-2	3.25
-1	3.5
0	4
1	5
2	7
3	11
4	19

x	$h\left(\frac{1}{4}x\right)$	$g(x)$
-8	$h\left(\frac{1}{4}\cdot -8\right) = h(-2)$	3.25
-4	$h\left(\frac{1}{4}\cdot -4\right) = h(-1)$	3.5
0		4
4		5
8		7
12		11
16		19

5. Consider the following table of values.

x	$f(x)$	$g(x)$	$h(x)$	$m(x)$
-5	25	23	-25	32
-3	9	7	-9	16
0	0	-2	0	7
3	9	7	-9	16
5	25	23	-25	32

Part A: Write $g(x)$ as a transformation of $f(x)$.

$$g(x) = f(x) - 2$$

Part B: Write $h(x)$ as a transformation of $f(x)$.

$$h(x) = -f(x)$$

Part C: Write $m(x)$ as a transformation of $f(x)$.

$$m(x) = f(x) + 7$$

6. Consider the following table of values.

x	$f(x)$
-5	25
-3	9
0	0
3	9
5	25

x	$m(x)$
-7	25
-5	9
-2	0
1	9
3	25

Part A: Write $m(x)$ as a transformation of $f(x)$.

$$m(x) = f(x+2)$$

Part B: Write $f(x)$ as a transformation of $m(x)$.

$$f(x) = m(x-2)$$

7. Consider the following graph.

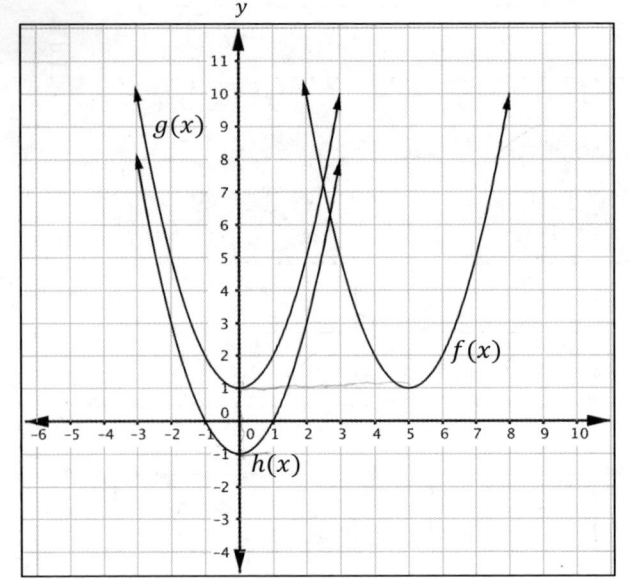

[Graph showing three parabolas: g(x) with vertex near (-2, 1), f(x) with vertex near (3, 1), and h(x) with vertex near (-2, -1)]

Part A: Write $h(x)$ as a transformation of $g(x)$.

$$h(x) = g(x) - 2$$

Part B: Write $g(x)$ as a transformation of $f(x)$.

$$g(x) = f(x+5)$$

Part C: Write $h(x)$ as a transformation of $f(x)$.

$$h(x) = f(x+5) - 2$$

8. Consider the following Algebra 1 standard that deals with transformations.

MAFS.912.F-BF.2.3: Identify the effect on the graph of replacing $f(x)$ by $f(x) + k$, $kf(x)$, $f(kx)$, and $f(x + k)$ for specific values of k (both positive and negative); find the value of k given the graphs.

Part A: Circle the expressions that describe a transformation on the independent variable.

$f(x+k)$ $f(kx)$

Part B: Underline the expressions that describe a transformation on the dependent variable.

$f(x) + k$ $kf(x)$

X = independent
Y = dependent

Section 4: Linear Equations, Functions, and Inequalities
Student Learning Plan

Topic Number	Topic Name	Date Completed	Study Expert(s)	Check Your Understanding Score
1	Arithmetic Sequences			
2	Rate of Change of Linear Functions			
3	Interpreting Rate of Change and y-intercept in a Real-World Context – Part 1			
4	Interpreting Rate of Change and y-intercept in a Real-World Context – Part 2			
5	Introduction to Systems of Equations			
6	Finding Solution Sets to Systems of Equations Using Substitution and Graphing			
7	Using Equivalent Systems of Equations			
8	Finding Solution Sets to Systems of Equations Using Elimination			
9	Solution Sets to Inequalities with Two Variables			
10	Finding Solution Sets to Systems of Linear Inequalities			

What did you learn in this section? What questions do you still have?

Who was your favorite Study Expert for this section? Why?

Practice Book - Section 4: Linear Equations, Functions, and Inequalities

Section 4 – Topic 1
Arithmetic Sequences

1. Describe the pattern in each sequence. Then find the next two terms of the sequence.

   Part A: $21, 16, 11, 6, 1, -4$

   Part B: $-3, 5, 13, 21, 29, 37$

   Part C: $72, 44, 16, -12, -40, -68$

2. State whether each sequence is arithmetic and justify your answer. If the sequence is arithmetic, write a recursive and an explicit formula to represent it.

   Part A: $52, 40, 28, 16$

   Part B: $2, 4, 8, 16, 32$

   Part C: $\frac{1}{4}, \frac{3}{4}, \frac{5}{4}, \frac{7}{4}, \frac{9}{4}$

   Part D: $1.1, 1.5, 1.9, 2.3, 2.7$

3. Find the third, fifth, and seventeenth terms of the sequence described by each explicit formula.

   Part A: $f(n) = 8 + 3(n-1)$

   Part B: $f(n) = 7 - 2(n-1)$

   Part C: $f(n) = 3 + \frac{n-1}{2}$

   Part D: $f(n) = -9.2 - 2.5(n-1)$

4. A theater has 50 seats on the front row. There are four additional seats in each following row.

   Part A: Write a rule to represent the number of seats in any given row as an explicit formula.

   Part B: How many seats are in the 20*th* row?

Practice Book - Section 4: Linear Equations, Functions, and Inequalities

5. Write an explicit formula for an arithmetic sequence whose common difference is −4.5.

6. Mississippi Live Streaming Weather Radio Broadcast from NOAA Weather Stations gives local weather updates every 18 minutes. The first update is at 2:00 p.m. You turn the radio on at 5:30 p.m.

   How long will you have to wait for the next local weather update?

7. The first term of an arithmetic sequence is 5. The eleventh term is 125.

   What is the common difference of the arithmetic sequence?

8. The city buses that run in your neighborhood stop every 12 minutes. The first bus arrives at 5:00 a.m. for passengers. You get to the bus stop at 8:37am.

   How long will you have to wait for a bus?

9. Faisal is conditioning all winter to prepare for his college's hockey team tryouts. He is incorporating barbell deadlifts into his daily workout regime. He plans to start with two reps and everyday he will complete two more reps than the day before.

   Part A: Write an explicit formula that can be used to find the number of reps lifted on any given day.

   Part B: If he starts with three reps on the first day, how many reps will he do on the 7th day of training?

Practice Book - Section 4: Linear Equations, Functions, and Inequalities

Section 4 – Topic 2
Rate of Change of Linear Functions

1. Jeff Mordon drives 140 miles in 4 hours.

   Part A: What is his rate of change?

   Part B: Represent the situation on the graph below.

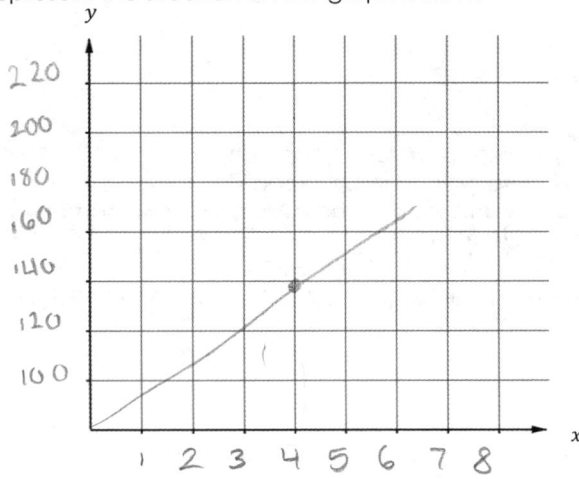

2. Claire and Rachel play volleyball for different teams. Claire's team practices seven hours every two days and Rachel's team practices eight hours every three days. Match each player to the graph that represents the average number of hours that they practice each day over a seven-day period.

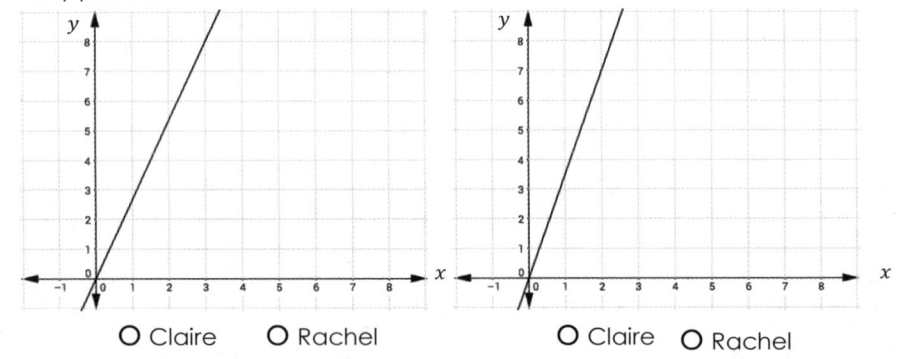

   ○ Claire   ○ Rachel   ○ Claire   ○ Rachel

3. Steve is trying to increase his average pace per mile by running hills. The hill on 1st Avenue rises 3 vertical feet for each horizontal foot. The hill on 16th Avenue rises 1 vertical foot for every 3 horizontal feet. Which hill will be more difficult for Steve to run up? Explain your reasoning.

4. The following graph represents the amount that Camila and Lydia charge for their babysitting services.

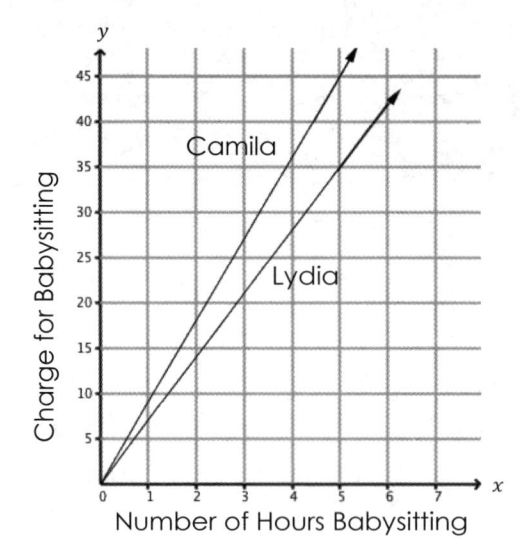

   Which of the following statements are true? Select all that apply.

   ☐ The rate of change of each line represents the amount each girl charges per hour for her babysitting services.
   ☐ Lydia's rate of change is greater than Camila's rate of change.
   ☐ Lydia's rate of change is $7 per hour.
   ☐ Camila charges $35 for 5 hours of babysitting services.
   ☐ Lydia charges $14 for 2 hours of babysitting services.

Practice Book - Section 4: Linear Equations, Functions, and Inequalities

5. Keon and Lesha are comparing their daily caloric intake. Each day, Lesha chooses healthy 100-calories snacks such as apples and carrots while Keon chooses snacks like chips and candy that have 200 calories each.

   Part A: Draw a graph to represent Keon's and Lesha's caloric intakes based on the number of snacks they eat, labeling each line and the axes.

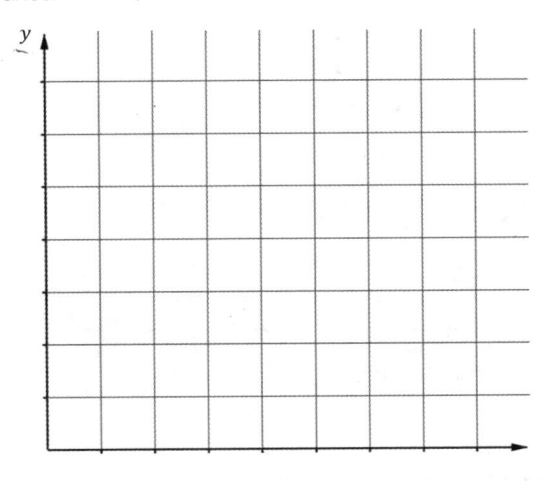

   Part B: What does the rate of change for each line represent?

   Part C: What is Lesha's rate of change?

   Part D: How does Lesha's rate of change compare to Keon's rate of change? Why are the two rates different from one another?

6. Steve repairs elevators. When he is called to a job he uses the stairwell to go to the floor on which the elevator is located. In the Modis building, he climbs 22 steps for every 15 feet of horizontal travel. In the Sears tower, he climbs 17 steps for every 7 feet of horizontal travel.

   Part A: What is the rate of change for each stairwell?

   Part B: Which stairwell will be easier to climb? Explain your reasoning.

7. J.K. Rowling and R.L. Stine are both reading *The Hunger Games*. J.K. reads 35 pages every 2 hours and R.L. reads 45 pages every 3 hours.

   Part A: What is the rate of change for each reader?

   Part B: If *The Hunger Games* is 355 pages, who will finish the book first?

8. José drives 65 miles per hour when he travels. Sherry drives 450 miles in 9 hours.

   Which driver has a faster rate of change?

Practice Book - Section 4: Linear Equations, Functions, and Inequalities

9. The following graph represents the money Matthew and Mitchell spend each hour when they play video games at the local arcade.

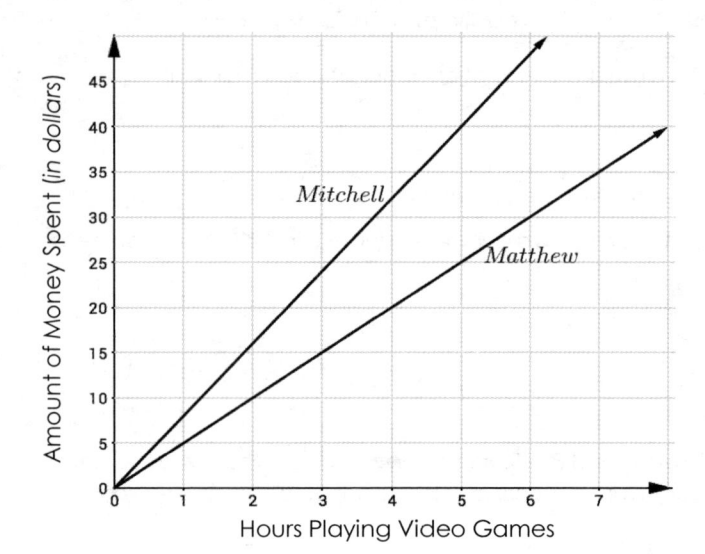

Which of the following statements are true? Select all that apply.

☐ Matthew is spending his money at a faster rate than Mitchell.
☐ The rate of change represents the money the boys spend per hour playing video games.
☐ Mitchell spends $3 every hour he plays video games.
☐ Matthew spends $8 every hour he plays video games.

10. Mrs. Cugini collected data on the hand span length and height of each of her Algebra 1 students. The graph below represents the scatterplot of the data for one class.

Part A: What is the slope of the graph?

Part B: What does the slope represent?

Section 4 – Topic 3
Interpreting Rate of Change and y – Intercept in a Real-World Context – Part 1

1. Appleseed, a tech company, spends a fixed cost of $1,500 to manufacture the wristbands for their new Appleseed Watch, plus $100 per unit manufactured.

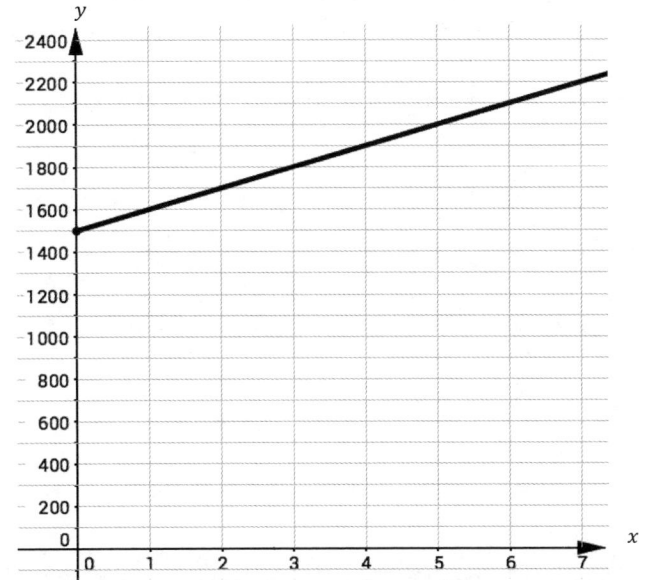

   Part A: What is the slope of the line? What does the slope represent?

   Part B: What is the y –intercept? What does the y –intercept represent?

2. You saved $300 to spend over the summer. You decide to budget $50 to spend each week.

   Part A: Write an equation that represents this situation.

   Part B: Represent the situation on the graph below.

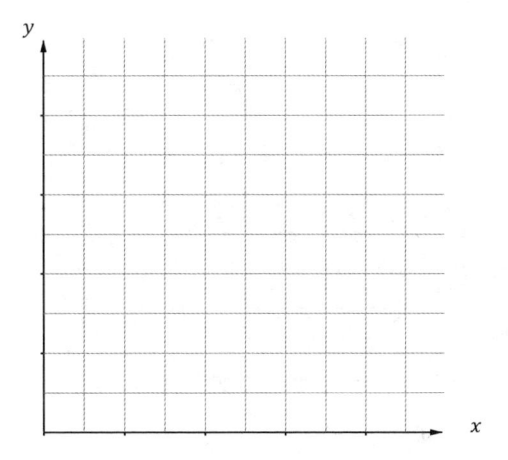

   Part C: What is the slope of the line? What does the slope represent?

   Part D: What is the y –intercept? What does this point represent?

Practice Book - Section 4: Linear Equations, Functions, and Inequalities

3. Consider the following graph.

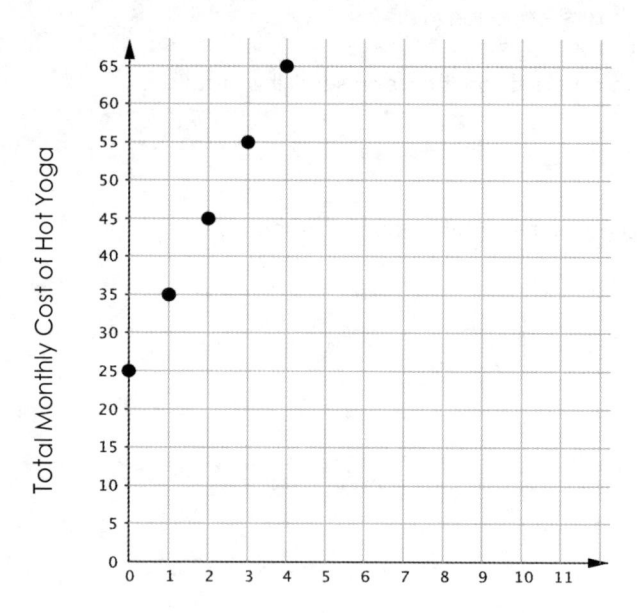

[Graph: Total Monthly Cost of Hot Yoga vs. Number of Hot Yoga Practices in a Month. Points plotted at approximately (0, 25), (1, 35), (2, 45), (3, 55), (4, 65).]

Number of Hot Yoga Practices in a Month

Part A: What is the slope of the line? What does the slope represent?

Part B: What is the y-intercept? What does the y-intercept represent?

Part C: Define the variables and write a function that represents this situation.

Part D: What does each point represent?

4. Consider the following standard:

CCSS.Math.Content.HSF-LE.5: Interpret the parameters in a linear or exponential function in terms of a context.

The parameters of a linear function are the slope and the y-intercept.

A cab company's fare can be modeled with the linear function $f(m) = 5 + 3m$, where m represents the number of miles for the rider's trip.

Describe the parameters and what they represent in this context.

Section 4 – Topic 4
Interpreting Rate of Change and y – Intercept in a Real-World Context – Part 2

1. Consider the following standard.

   > Interpret the parameters in a linear or exponential function in terms of a context.

   In the equation $y = mx + b$, identify which letters represent the two parameters of the linear function.

2. Consider the following equations.

   Equation A: $2x + 3y = 12$
   Equation B: $2x + 3y = 6$

   How will the graphs of the two equations differ from each other?

3. Consider the equation $y = 3x - 1$. Identify the slope and y–intercept and sketch the graph.

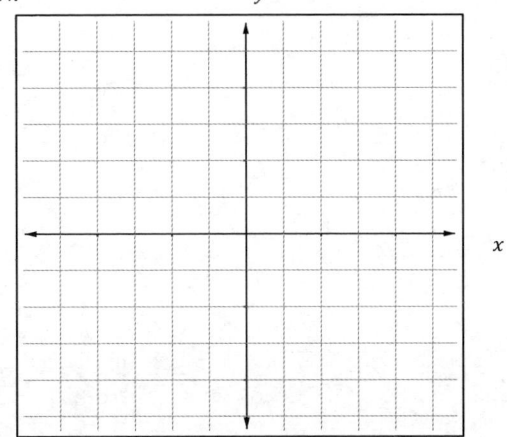

4. Consider the equation, $3x + 4y = 12$.

   Part A: Write the equation in slope-intercept form.

   Part B: Identify the y–intercept.

   Part C: Identify the slope.

   Part D: Graph the equation.

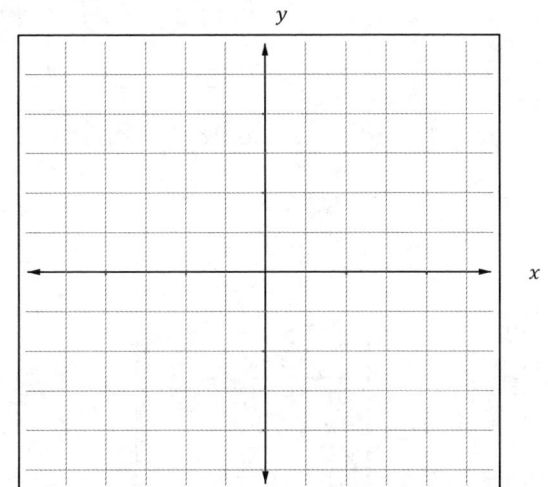

5. Consider the equation $-2x + 3y = 6$.

   Part A: Write the equation in slope-intercept form.

   Part B: Identify the y–intercept.

   Part C: Identify the slope.

Part D: Graph the equation.

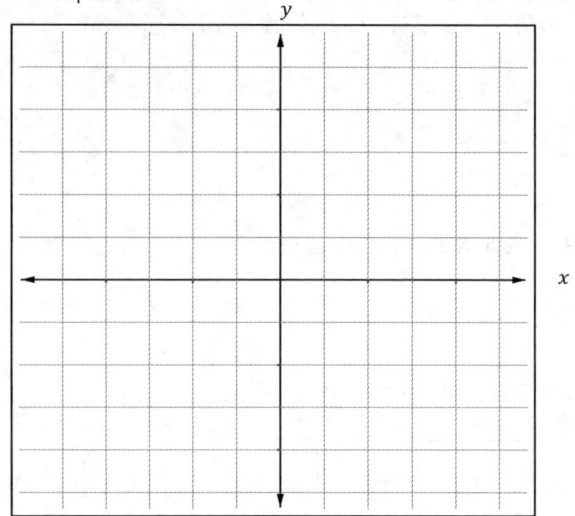

6. Line z, $\triangle QUT$, and $\triangle RVS$ are shown on the coordinate plane below.

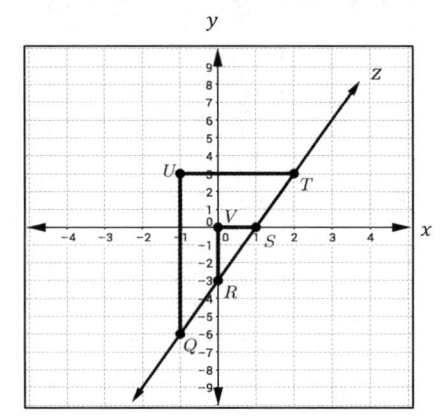

Which of the following statements are true? Select all that apply.

☐ The slope of line z is equal to $\frac{TU}{QU}$.
☐ The slope of line z is equal to $\frac{RV}{SV}$.
☐ The slope of line z is equal to $\frac{RV}{TV}$.
☐ The slope of $\overline{QR}$ is equal to the slope of $\overline{ST}$.
☐ The slope of $\overline{RS}$ is equal to the slope of line z.
☐ The y-intercept of line z is 1.
☐ Line z represents a continuous function.

7. Line h is shown on the coordinate plane below.

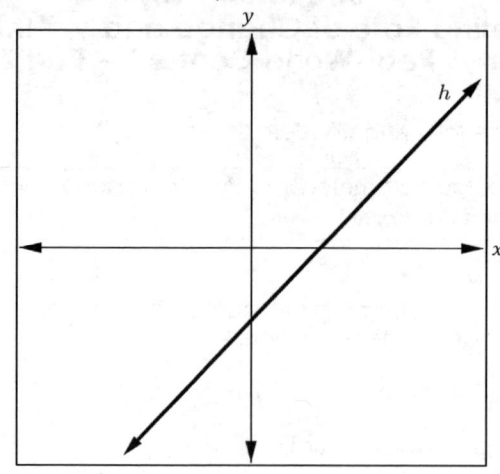

Which statement is true about line h?

Ⓐ The slope is less than 0 and the y–intercept is greater than zero.
Ⓑ The slope is less than 0 and the y–intercept is less than zero.
Ⓒ The slope is greater than 0 and the y–intercept is greater than zero.
Ⓓ The slope is greater than 0 and the y–intercept is less than zero.

Practice Book - Section 4: Linear Equations, Functions, and Inequalities

Section 4 – Topic 5
Introduction to Systems of Equations

1. Consider the following system of equations.

    Line 1: $3x + y = 6$

    Line 2: $3x - y = 6$

    Part A: Graph the system of equations below.

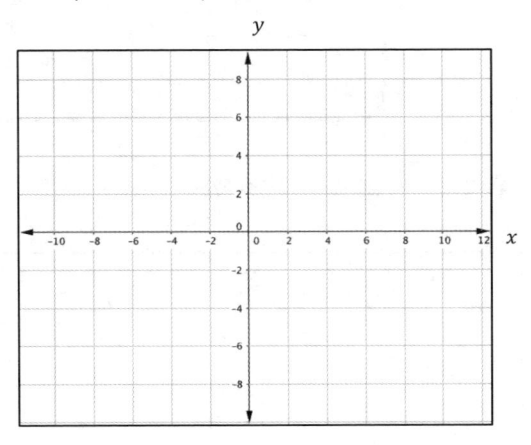

    Part B: What is the solution to the system of equations?

    Part C: Explain how you know it is the solution.

2. Consider the following system of equations.

    Line 1: $2x - y = -3$

    Line 2: $-6x - 2y = -6$

    Part A: Is $(0, 3)$ a solution to Line 1? Explain your answer.

    Part B: Coordinate $(0, -3)$ is a solution to Line 2.

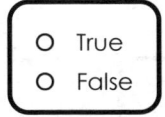

    ○ True
    ○ False

    Part C: What are the slopes of Line 1 and Line 2?

    Part D: What are the y-intercepts of Line 1 and Line 2?

    Part E: Sketch the graph of Line 1 and Line 2.

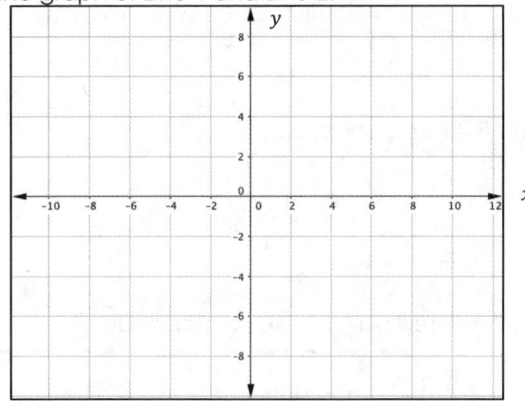

    Part F: What is the solution to the system?

Practice Book - Section 4: Linear Equations, Functions, and Inequalities

3. Consider the following system of equations.

$$\text{Line 1: } x + y = -2$$
$$\text{Line 2: } 3x - y = 2$$

Part A: The ordered pair $(-4, 2)$ is a solution to
- ○ Line 1.
- ○ Line 2.
- ○ the system of equations.

Part B: The ordered pair $(2, 4)$ is a solution to
- ○ Line 1.
- ○ Line 2.
- ○ the system of equations.

Part C: The ordered pair $(0, -2)$ is a solution to
- ○ Line 1.
- ○ Line 2.
- ○ the system of equations.

Part D: What does the solution to this system of equations represent?

4. Consider the following equation

$$\text{Line 1: } x - y = 9$$
$$\text{Line 2: } 3x + 3y = 3$$

Part A: The ordered pair $(3, -6)$ is a solution to
- ○ Line 1.
- ○ Line 2.
- ○ the system of equations.

Part B: The ordered pair $(-1, 1)$ is a solution to
- ○ both.
- ○ neither.
- ○ the system of equations.

Part C: The ordered pair $(5, -4)$ is a solution to
- ○ Line 1.
- ○ Line 2.
- ○ the system of equations.

Part D: Sketch the graph of the system.

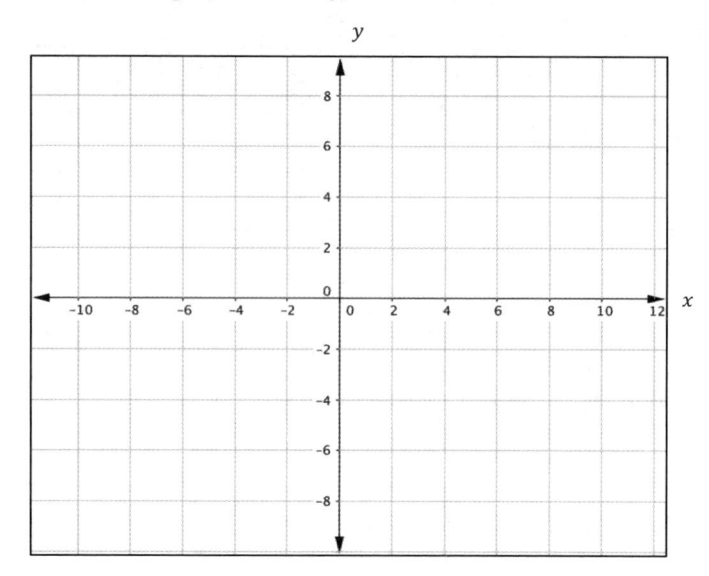

Section 4 – Topic 6
Finding Solution Sets to Systems of Equations Using Substitution and Graphing

1. Last Monday, two law students met up at Café Literatura after school to read the pages they were assigned in the Legal Methods class. Alejandro can read 1 page per minute, and he has read 28 pages so far. Carly, who has a reading speed of 2 pages per minute, has read 12 pages so far.

   Part A: Define the variables and write two equations to represent the number of pages that each student read.

   Variables:

   Alejandro:

   Carly:

   Part B: Represent the two equations on the graph below.

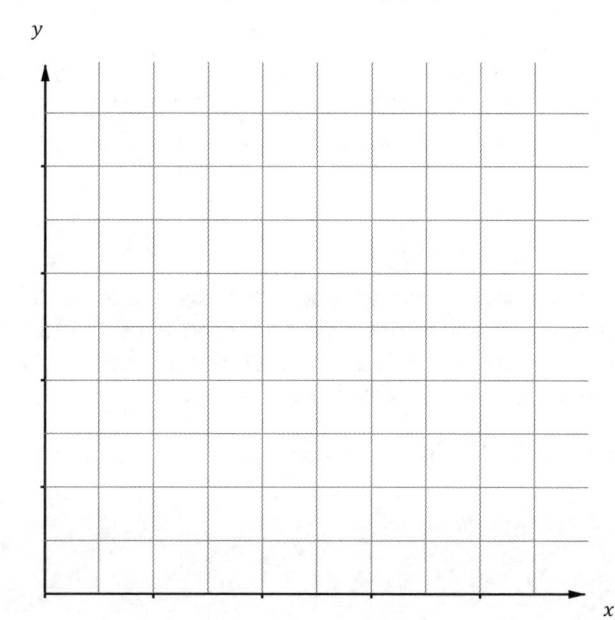

   Part C: What is the rate of change for each student?

   Part D: What does the rate of change represent in this situation?

   Part E: What is the y –intercept for Alejandro? What does it represent?

   Part F: What is the y –intercept for Carly? What does it represent?

   Part G: Give an example when Alejandro has read more pages than Carly. Justify your answer.

   Part H: Use the substitution method to determine when Alejandro and Carly have read the same number of pages.

2. Parabola Skate Rental rents skate boards for $4.50 per hour with a rental fee of $35. Arc of Hawk Skate Rental rents skate boards for $5.25 per hour with a rental fee of $25.

   Part A: Define the variables and write two equations to represent each rental company.

   Variables:

   Parabola:

   Arc of Hawk:

   Part B: Represent the two equations on the graph below.

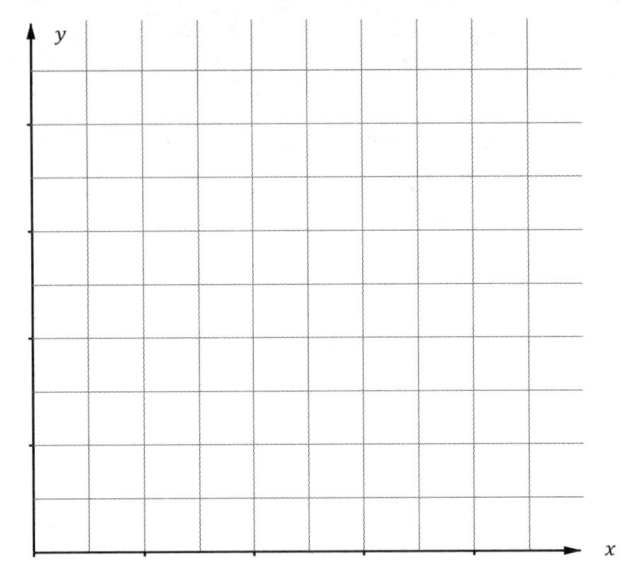

   Part C: What is the rate of change for each rental company?

   Parabola:

   Arc of Hawk:

   Part D: What does the rate of change represent in this situation?

   Part E: What are the y–intercepts of each graph and what do they represent?

   Parabola:

   Arc of Hawk:

   Part F: Give an example of when renting from Parabola's would be a better deal than renting from Arc of Hawk's? Justify your answer.

   Part G: Use the substitution method to help the renter determine when the two skate board rentals will cost the same amount.

3. In a basketball game, Tatiana made 23 baskets. Each of the baskets was worth either 2 or 3 points, and Tatiana scored a total of 53 points. Let x represent the number of two-point baskets she made and y represent the number of three-point baskets she made.

   Part A: Write a system of equations to represent the situation.

Part B: Would you use graphing or substitution to solve the system and determine the number of two-point and three-point baskets Tatiana made? Explain.

Part C: Use the method you chose in Part B to solve the system and find out how many two-point and three-point baskets Tatiana made.

4. The graph below shows a system of equations:

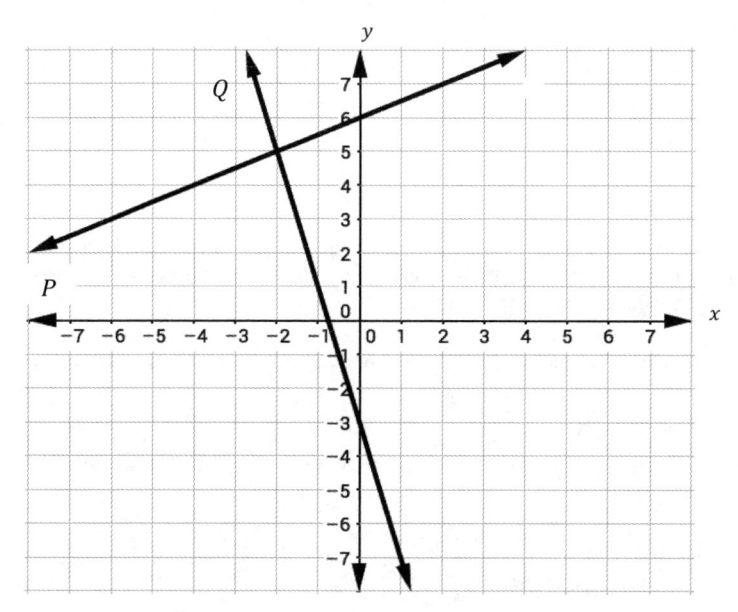

Part A: Write the equation of each line in slope-intercept form.

Line P:

Line Q:

Part B: What is the solution to the system?

5. You are trying to decide which cell phone plan to purchase. Plan A charges $40 for a new phone and $20 a month for usage. Plan B provides the phone for free but has a fee of $30 a month for usage.

Part A: Write an equation to represent each plan.

Plan A:

Plan B:

Part B: Represent the two plans on the graph below.

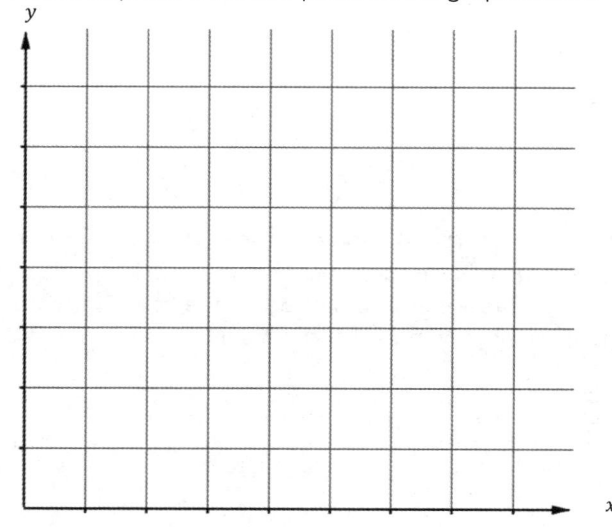

Practice Book - Section 4: Linear Equations, Functions, and Inequalities

Part C: Use the substitution method to determine when the two plans will cost the same.

6. Monroe and Kalyani solved the following system:

$$y = 3x + 1$$
$$y = -x + 5$$

Monroe used substitution and found the solution set to be (1,4) while Kalyani graphed and found the solution set to be (2,7).

Part A: How would you determine who is correct?

Part B: Whose solution set is correct?

7. Traci is running a trail in Hanna Park. She can run one mile in ten minutes. Yoni is running the same trail as Traci. Yoni can run a mile in five minutes but starts running 20 minutes after Traci started on the trail. If they start the trail from the same point, how long will it take Yoni to catch up with Traci?

8. Mr. Gardner is contemplating which shuttle service to take to the airport. Fast Shuttle charges a $5 pick-up fee and $0.25 per mile. Steady Shuttle charges a $2 pick-up fee and $0.50 per mile.

Part A: When will the two plans cost the same amount?

Part B: If the airport is 20 miles away, which company should Mr. Gardner choose?

9. Maggie makes and sells scented body lotions. She initially spent $108 to purchase supplies, and each kilogram of lotion costs $16 to make. Maggie sells the lotion for $25 per kilogram.

How many kilograms of lotion will Maggie have to sell to break even?

Section 4 – Topic 7
Using Equivalent Systems of Equations

1. Consider the equation $2x + 2y = 8$.

   Part A: Write an equivalent equation by multiplying the equation by 3. Does the equation have the same solution set? Use www.Desmos.com to check your answer.

   Part B: Write an equivalent equation by dividing the equation by 2. Does the equation have the same solution set? Use www.Desmos.com to check your answer.

2. Consider the following system that has a solution of (5,3).

$$\begin{cases} x + y = 8 & Equation\ 1 \\ x - y = 2 & Equation\ 2 \end{cases}$$

   Complete the following table by performing the operations to write equivalent systems. Use www.Desmos.com to verify that the systems have the same solution.

Operation to Perform	Equivalent System	Solution
Multiply Equation 1 by 4. Keep Equation 2 the same.		
Keep Equation 1 the same. Add Equation 1 and Equation 2.		
Subtract Equation 2 from Equation 1. Keep Equation 2 the same.		
Multiply the sum of Equation 1 and Equation 2 by 3. Keep Equation 2 the same.		

3. Given a system of equations, list three ways that we can write new equations that can be used to create equivalent systems.

4. Consider the following system which has a solution of $(-1, 4)$ and Q, R, S, T, U and V are non-zero real numbers:

$$\begin{cases} Qx + Ry = S \\ Tx + Uy = V \end{cases}$$

   Write two new equations that could be used to create an equivalent system of equations.

5. The system $\begin{cases} Ax + By = C \\ Mx + Ny = P \end{cases}$ has solution $(2, 3)$, where $A, B, C, M, N,$ and P are non-zero real numbers. Select all the systems of equations with the same solution.

   ☐ $\begin{cases} (A + M)x + (B + N)y = C + P \\ Mx + Ny = P \end{cases}$

   ☐ $\begin{cases} (A + M)x + By = C + P \\ Mx + (N + B)y = P \end{cases}$

   ☐ $\begin{cases} Ax + By = C \\ (2A + M)x + (2B + N)y = 2C + P \end{cases}$

   ☐ $\begin{cases} Ax + By = C \\ (M - A)x + (N - B)y = P - C \end{cases}$

   ☐ $\begin{cases} Ax + By = C \\ 4Mx + 4Ny = 4P \end{cases}$

Section 4 – Topic 8
Finding Solution Sets to Systems of Equations Using Elimination

1. Laneka owns a cake shop. She is currently preparing cakes for two anniversary parties. The first cake has 3 small tiers and 1 medium tier and will serve a total of 100 guests. The second one has 3 small tiers and 2 medium tiers and will serve a total of 140 guests.

   Part A: Represent the situation with a system of equations.

   Part B: Solve the system of equations.

   Part C: How many guests will a small tier and medium tier serve?

2. During their last game, the Miami Dolphins scored 6 times for a total score of 30 points. They scored 7 points for each touchdown and 3 points for each field goal.

   Write and solve the systems of equations to find the total touchdowns and field goals scored.

3. Laura and Luis are hosting a FIFA World Cup Finals party and have purchased dinnerware to represent their favorite teams. Lara, a fan of team Germany, bought 25 cups and 40 plates with the German flag printed on them. Luis, who is rooting for Argentina, bought 20 cups and 35 plates with the Argentinian flag printed on them. Laura spent a total of $445.00 and Luis spent a total of $380.00.

   Which of the following systems could represent the situation? Select all that apply.

   ☐ $25c + 40p = 445$
   ☐ $25c + 25c = 445$
   ☐ $20c + 35p = 380$
   ☐ $35p + 40p = 380$
   ☐ $45c + 75p = 825$

4. Rigo and Ian went shopping for soccer cleats and practice uniforms. Rigo spent $451, before taxes, and purchased three uniforms and one pair of cleats. Ian spent $757, before taxes, and purchased five uniforms and two pairs of cleats.

   Part A: Assuming all the uniforms cost the same amount and all the cleats cost the same amount, write a system of equations to represent each boy's total purchases.

   Part B: Use the elimination method to find the price of each uniform and each pair of cleats.

5. Marina volunteers at the Salvation Army. She has been tasked with buying non-perishable items for families that were displaced by a recent flood. She finds a company willing to sell her cans of food at a discounted price. In the system below, x represents the number of small cans she purchased and y represents the number of large cans she purchased.

$$2.25x + 4.75y = 714.75$$
$$x + y = 181$$

Part A: How many cans did Marina purchase?

Part B: What was the total amount Marina spent on the purchase?

Part C: How many small cans did Marina purchase?

Part D: How many large cans did Marina purchase?

Part E: How much does a small can cost?

Part F: How much does a large can cost?

6. The sum of two different integers is 7. The following system represents the two integers.

$$x + y = 7$$
$$3x + 2y = 46$$

Which of the following statements about the solutions to the system is true? Select all that apply.

☐ There are infinite solutions to the system since there are infinitely many integers whose sum is 7.
☐ There are two solutions to the system, one that satisfies the first equation and a second solution that satisfies the second equation.
☐ The two solutions are $(3, 4)$ and $(10, 8)$.
☐ There is exactly one solution to the system that satisfies both equations.
☐ The solution to the equation is $(32, -25)$.
☐ There is no solution to the system since there is no solution that would satisfy both equations.

7. Colossal Elementary School had a mother/daughter painting weekend. On Saturday, eight mothers worked with 12 daughters to paint 220 square feet of a large mural on a wall in the gymnasium. The next day, six moms worked with eight daughters to paint another 152 square feet of the mural in the gym.

Write and solve a system of equations to find how many square feet each mom painted and how many square feet each daughter painted. Assume all moms painted at the same rate and all daughters painted at the same rate.

8. Fill in the missing operation or missing equation to complete the table.

Solve by elimination $\begin{cases} 5x - 2y = 17 \\ 3x + 7y = 43 \end{cases}$

Operations	Equations	Labels
	$\begin{cases} 5x - 2y = 17 \\ 3x + 7y = 43 \end{cases}$	Equation 1 Equation 2
	$-15x + 6y = -51$	New Equation 1
Multiply Equation 2 by 5.		New Equation 2
	$-15x + 6y = -51$ $15x + 35y = 215$ $\overline{41y = 164}$	
Divide by 41.		
Solve for x.		
Write x and y as coordinates.		Solution to the system

Section 4 – Topic 9
Solution Sets to Inequalities with Two Variables

1. Stacy's mom is baking treats for Stacy's birthday party. She has 9 eggs to use for this purpose. A batch of cookies requires one egg and a batch of brownies requires 2 eggs. How many of each treat can Stacy's mom bake?

   Part A: List three possible combinations of cookies and brownies Stacy's mom could make for the party.

   Part B: Write an inequality to represent the situation.

   Part C: Graph the inequality and shade the area where the solutions are.

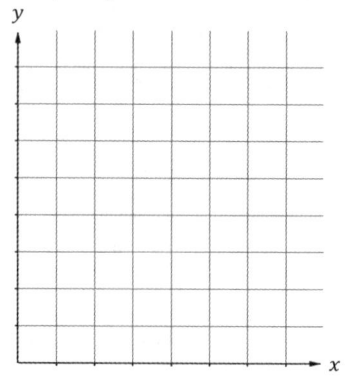

   Part D: Why did we only graph in the first quadrant?

68 Practice Book - Section 4: Linear Equations, Functions, and Inequalities

2. Jessie's daughter went to Target and bought $1 or $2 items from the One Spot area. She wants to spend less than $20 at Target.

   Part A: List three possible combinations of $1 or $2 items she could buy.

   Part B: Write an inequality to represent the situation.

   Part C: Graph the inequality and shade the area where the solutions are.

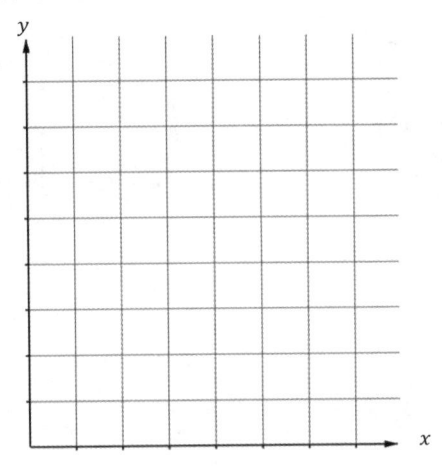

   Part D: What is the difference between the ordered pairs that fall on the line and the ones that fall in the shaded area?

3. The lacrosse team is raising money by selling cheesecakes. The players plan to sell an entire cheesecake for $24.00 each and slices of cheesecake for $3.50 each. If they want to raise at least $700, how many of each could they sell?

   Part A: List three possible combinations of entire cheesecakes and slices of cheesecake the players could sell to reach their goal of raising at least $700.

   Part B: Write an inequality to represent the situation.

   Part C: Graph the inequality and shade where the solutions are.

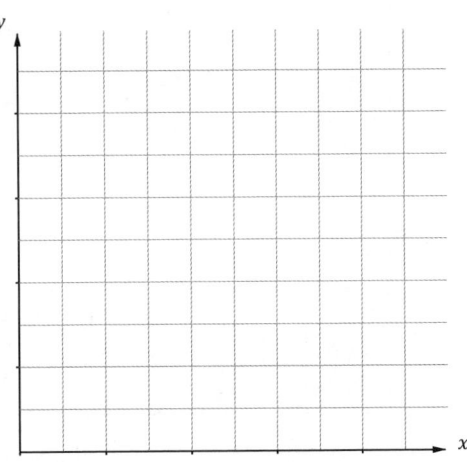

   Part D: What is the difference in the amount of money raised for ordered pairs falling on the line and the ones that fall in the shaded area?

   Part E: What do the x- and y-intercepts represent?

Practice Book - Section 4: Linear Equations, Functions, and Inequalities

4. At Dancing Coefficients Academy, each dance class is performing in the academy's talent show. The contemporary dance class presentation must be less than 35 minutes. They decide to have a combination of songs by Jason Mraz and Corry Crowder. Each Jason Mraz song lasts three and a half minutes and each Corey Crowder song lasts five minutes.

Part A: Write an inequality to represent the situation.

Part B: Graph the inequality and shade the area where the solutions are.

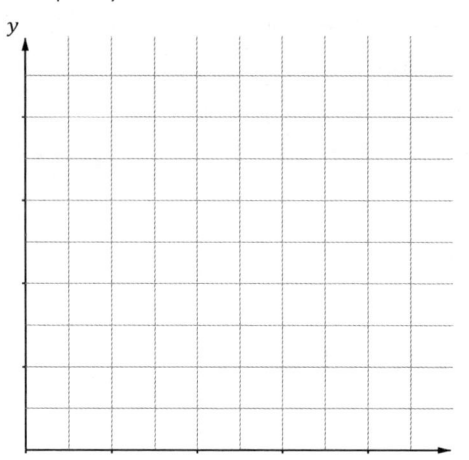

5. Which graph represents the solution set to the inequality $y < x - 4$?

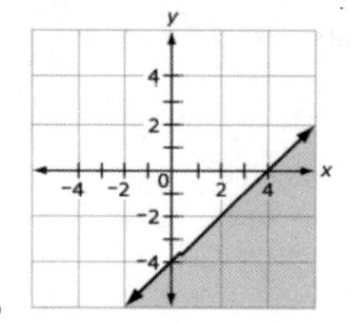

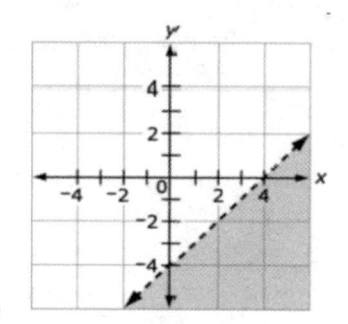

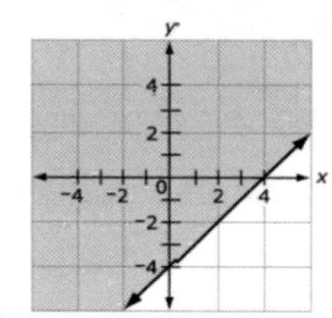

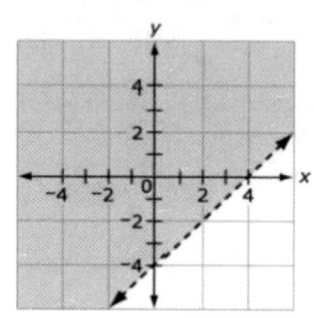

Ⓐ

Ⓑ

Ⓒ

Ⓓ

6. Nelson is fixing up his office and must spend less than $7,500 to hire carpenters and painters. Carpenters charge $28 per hour and painters charge $32 per hour.

   Part A: Write an inequality to represent the situation.

   Part B: If he hires a carpenter for 40 hours, what is the maximum number of hours the painter can work without exceeding his budget?

7. Bailey is inviting people to her wedding and has a budget of $4,500 for the food. The cost will be $65 for each adult's meal and $20 for each child's meal.

   Part A: Write an inequality to represent the situation.

   Part B: If there are 63 adults coming, what is the maximum number of children that can attend? Why?

8. Sabrina is catering a friend's party. A pan of chicken will feed 28 guests and a tray of turkey wraps will feed 42 guests. In total, the food must feed at least 428 guests.

   Part A: Write an inequality to represent the situation.

   Part B: If she prepares 7 pans of chicken, what is the minimum number of trays of turkey wraps she must prepare for the party? Why?

Section 4 – Topic 10
Finding Solution Sets to Systems of Linear Inequalities

1. Latisha wants to buy pumpkins and autumn squash for a fall display. She has a budget of no more than $117 but wants to buy more than 10 vegetables for the decorations. The pumpkins are $5.50 each and the autumn squash are $3.50 each.

   Part A: Write a system of linear inequalities to represent the situation.

   Part B: List three possible combinations of pumpkins and squash that Latisha can purchase to represent the situation.

   Part C: If Latisha decides she is going to use 12 pumpkins for the display, what is the maximum number of squash she can use?

2. Rasheed is buying wings and quesadillas for a party. A package of wings costs $8. A package of quesadillas costs $10. He must spend no more than $160. Rasheed's freezer will hold a maximum of 20 packages of wings and quesadillas.

   Part A: Write a system of linear inequalities to represent the situation.

Part B: Graph the system of linear inequalities and shade where the solutions are.

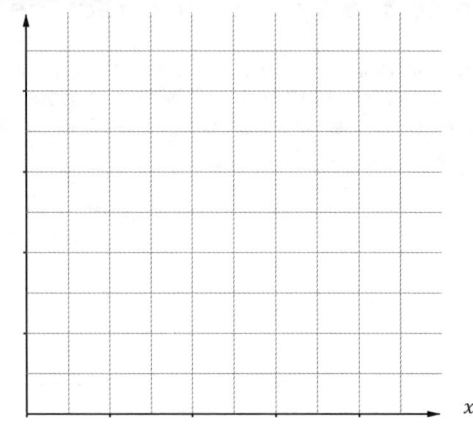

Part C: Which of the following combinations satisfy the situation above? Select all that apply.

☐ 10 packages of wings and 9 packages of quesadillas

☐ 5 packages of wings and 13 packages of quesadillas

☐ 5 packages of wings 12 packages of quesadillas

☐ 13 packages of wings 7 packages of quesadillas

☐ 9 packages of wings 8 packages of quesadillas

☐ 14 packages of wings 7 packages of quesadillas

Part D: If Rasheed buys 7 packages of wings, what is the maximum number of packages of quesadillas he can buy? Why?

3. Nivyana and Ana are selling their apparel to earn money for a cruise. Knitted scarves are $50 each, and mittens are $25 per pair. They cannot make more than 30 scarves and mittens combined. They need to earn at least $1,000 to pay for the cruise and souvenirs.

Part A: Write the inequalities that would represent the situation.

Part B: Graph the system of linear inequalities and shade where the solutions are.

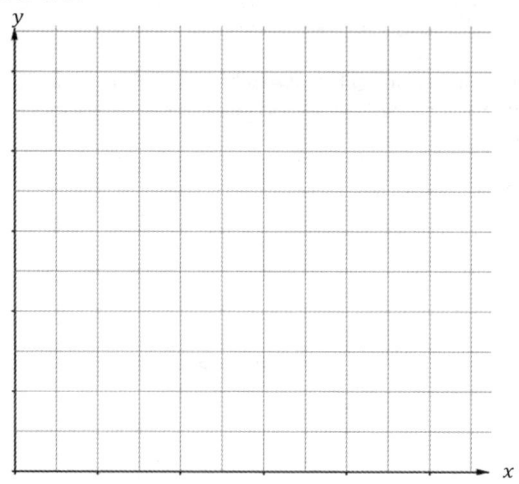

Part C: Identify two possible solutions to Nivyana and Ana's situation.

_____ scarves   _____ scarves

_____ mittens   _____ mittens

4. Your time spent playing pool and ice skating must not exceed 20 hours a week. Your weekly allowance is $80. You pay $3 an hour playing pool and $5 an hour for ice skating.

   Part A: Write the inequalities that represent the situation.

   Part B: Graph the system of linear inequalities and shade where the solutions are.

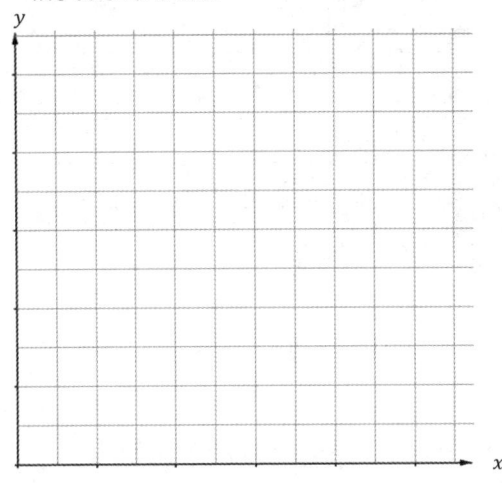

   Part C: Identify two possible solutions to this situation.

   _____ hours playing pool   _____ hours playing pool

   _____ hours ice skating   _____ hours ice skating

5. Consider the following graph that represents a system of inequalities and its boundary lines.

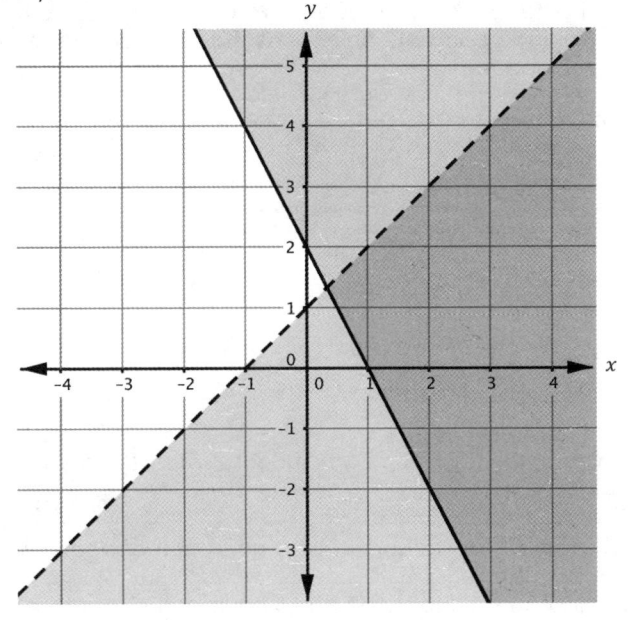

   Part A: Write three ordered pairs in the solution of this system.

   Part B: Write the inequalities that this graph represents.

Practice Book - Section 4: Linear Equations, Functions, and Inequalities

6. Every week, Rolando works at Starbucks during the day and at a youth soccer league at night. He can work a maximum of 40 hours a week. He calculates he needs to earn at least $368 every week to cover his expenses. Rolando earns $13 an hour at Starbucks and $9 an hour at the youth soccer league.

   Part A: Write a system of linear inequalities to represent the situation.

   Part B: Which of the following combinations satisfy the situation above? Select all that apply.

   ☐ 32 hours at Starbucks and 9 hours at the soccer league

   ☐ 30 hours at Starbucks and 5 hours at the soccer league

   ☐ 25 hours at Starbucks and 4 hours at the soccer league

   ☐ 19 hours at Starbucks and 13 hours at the soccer league

   ☐ 15 hours at Starbucks and 20 hours at the soccer league

   ☐ 10 hours at Starbucks and 26 hours at the soccer league

   Part C: If Rolando works 22 hours at Starbucks, what is the minimum number of hours he needs to work at the youth soccer league to cover his expenses? Why?

7. Fabiola is reviewing for the Algebra 1 End-of-Course exam. She made this graph representing a system of inequalities.

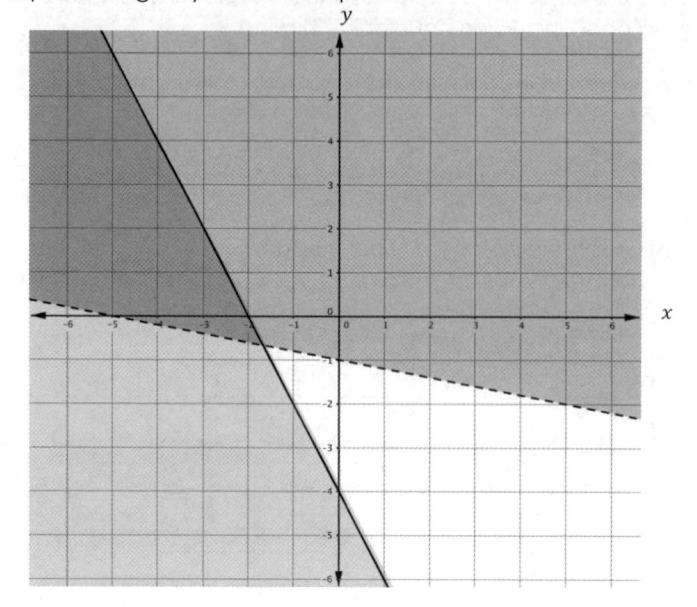

   Part A: Circle the ordered pairs below that represent solutions to the system of inequalities.

   $(-6, 3)$ $(-3, 3)$ $(0, 3)$ $(0, 0)$ $(6, 0)$

   $(-6, -6)$ $(-3, -6)$ $(-6, 6)$ $(-4, 2)$ $(3, -3)$

   Part B: Write the inequalities that this graph represents.

8. Create a storyline (word problem) for the real-world graph below.

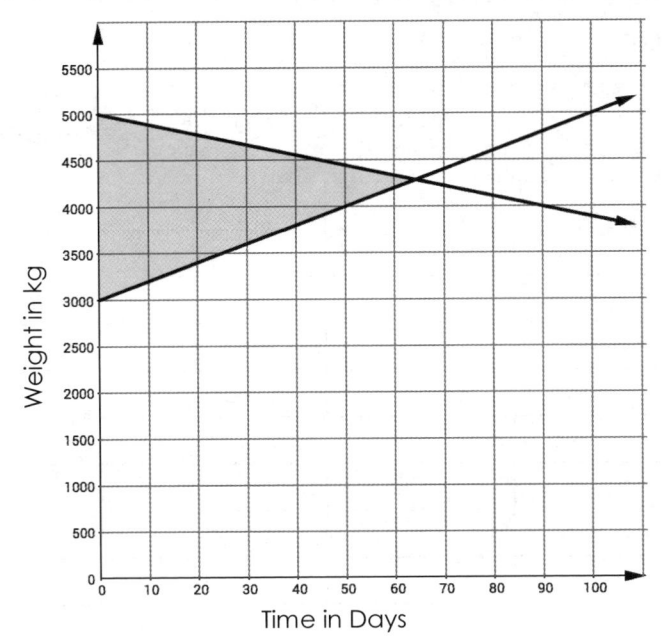

9. Write and solve a system of inequalities for the shaded region described. The shaded region is a triangle with vertices at $(-3, 0), (3, 2),$ and $(0, -2)$.

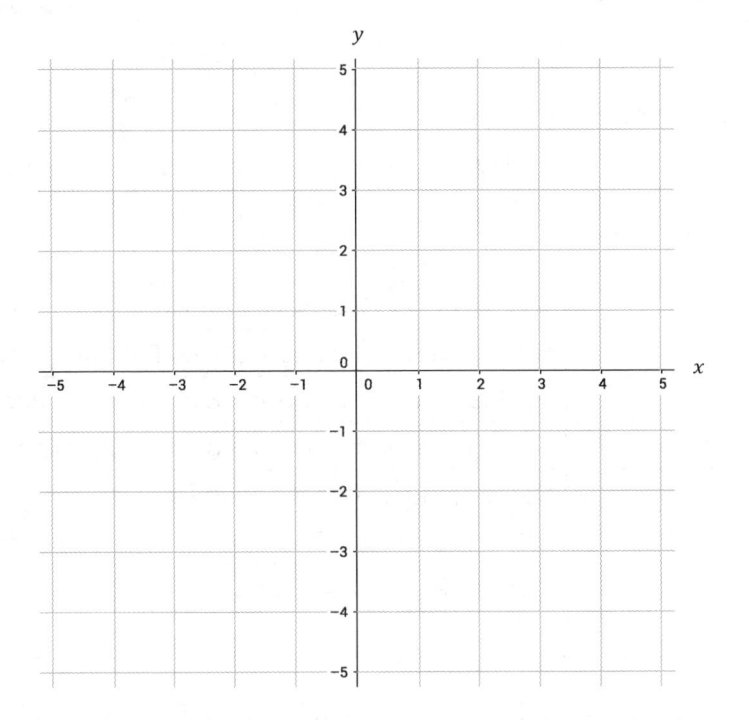

Practice Book - Section 4: Linear Equations, Functions, and Inequalities

Section 5: Quadratic Equations and Functions – Part 1
Student Learning Plan

Topic Number	Topic Name	Date Completed	Study Expert(s)	Check Your Understanding Score
1	Real-World Examples of Quadratic Functions			
2	Factoring Quadratic Expressions			
3	Solving Quadratic Equations by Factoring			
4	Solving Other Quadratic Equations by Factoring			
5	Solving Quadratic Equations by Factoring – Special Cases			
6	Solving Quadratic Equations by Taking Square Roots			
7	Solving Quadratic Equations by Completing the Square			
8	Deriving the Quadratic Formula			
9	Solving Quadratic Equations Using the Quadratic Formula			
10	Quadratic Functions in Action			
Honors 1	Polynomial Identities			

*Honors resources are available online.

What did you learn in this section? What questions do you still have?

Who was your favorite Study Expert for this section? Why?

Section 5 – Topic 1
Real-World Examples of Quadratic Functions

1. The function below shows the revenue for t-shirt sales. For every $1 decrease in price, 5 more t-shirts can be sold.

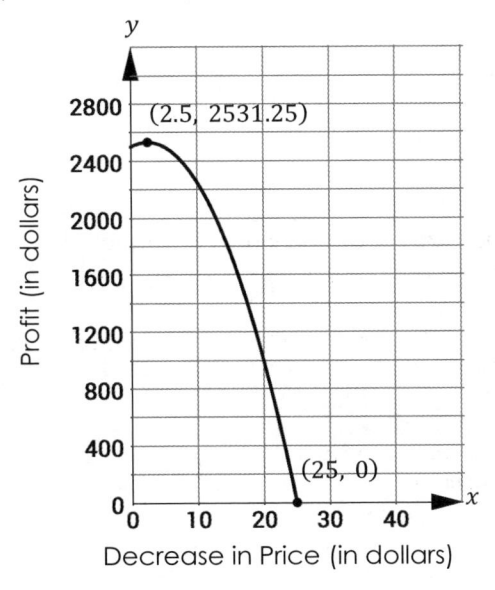

   (2.5, 2531.25)
   (25, 0)

   Decrease in Price (in dollars)
   Profit (in dollars)

   Part A: What it the maximum of this graph and what does the maximum represent?

   Part B: What is the y-intercept of the graph? What does it represent?

   Part C: Does the graph have solution(s)? If so, identify the solution and what it represents.

2. The height over time graph of a ball being dropped from the third story of a building is shown below.

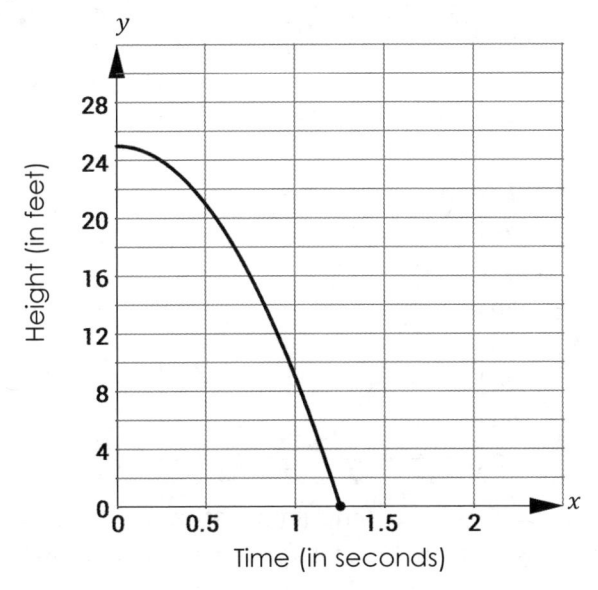

   Time (in seconds)
   Height (in feet)

   Part A: What is the maximum of this graph and what does it represent?

   Part B: What is the y-intercept of the graph? What does it represent?

   Part C: Does the graph have solution(s)? If so, identify the solution and what it represents.

Practice Book - Section 5: Quadratic Equations and Functions - Part 1

3. The height over time graph of a bungee jump is shown below.

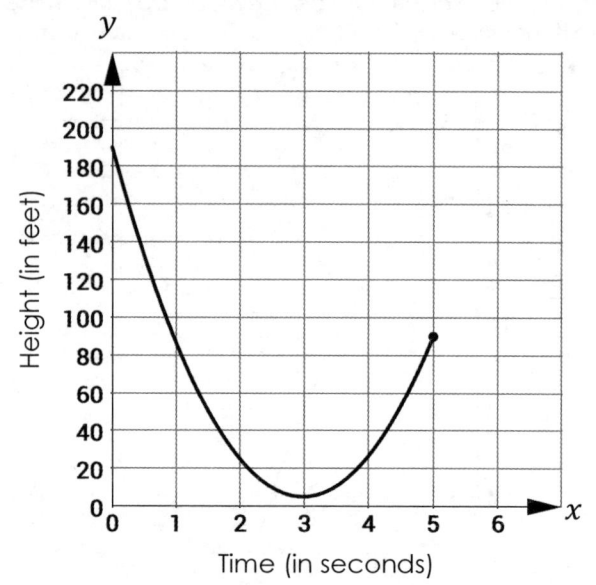

Part A: What is the minimum of this graph and what does it represent?

Part B: What is the y-intercept of the graph? What does it represent?

Part C: Does the graph have solution(s)? If so, identify the solution and what it represents.

4. Describe two real-world situations that could be modeled by a quadratic function.

Section 5 – Topic 2
Factoring Quadratic Expressions

1. Identify all factors of the expression $4x^2 + 17x - 15$.
   - ☐ 2
   - ☐ 3
   - ☐ $x - 5$
   - ☐ $x + 5$
   - ☐ $4x - 3$
   - ☐ $4x + 3$

2. A rectangular skateboard park has an area of $x^2 + 15x + 56$. What are possible dimensions of the park?

3. Match the expression in Column A with its definition in Column B using the following equation.

$$x^2 + 5x - 84 = (x + 12)(x - 7)$$

Column A	Column B
$(x + 12)(x - 7)$	factors of –84
$x^2 + 5x - 84$	sum of 12 and –7
12 and –7	trinomial
5	factored form of $x^2 + 5x - 84$

78

Practice Book - Section 5: Quadratic Functions - Part 1

4. List two possible values of c given the following values of b, for $x^2 + bx + c$ if $c > 0$.

   Part A: $b = -7$

   Part B: $b = -3$

   Part C: $b = 6$

   Part D: $b = 12$

5. Use the numbers below.

   | −9 | −6 | −1 | 2 | 3 | 4 | 7 |

   Which number makes each equation below true?

   $n^2 + 6n + 8 = (n + 2)(n + \square)$ _____

   $n^2 - 16n + 63 = (n - 7)(n + \square)$ _____

   $\square n^2 - 17n + 14 = (2n + 7)(-3n + 2)$ _____

   $v^2 - 3v - 18 = (v - 6)(v + \square)$ _____

   $2v^2 + 10v + 12 = \square(v + 2)(v + 3)$ _____

   $14x^2 + 17x + 5 = (\square x + 5)(2x + 1)$ _____

   $5x^2 - x - 4 = (5x + 4)(x + \square)$ _____

6. What are the possible values of b for the following values of c, for $x^2 + bx + c$ if $b > 0$?

   Part A: $c = -7$

   Part B: $c = -3$

   Part C: $c = 6$

   Part D: $c = 12$

7. The area of a rectangular garden is $2g^2 + 34g + 140$. If the width is $2g + 14$, what is the length?

8. Consider the quadratic expression $t^2 + 4t - 77$.

   Part A: Factor using the area model.

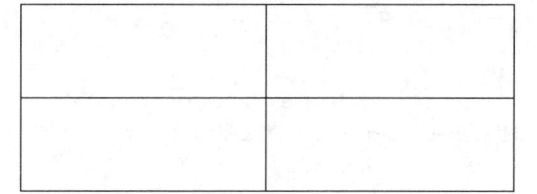

   Part B: Factor using the distributive property.

Section 5 – Topic 3
Solving Quadratic Equations by Factoring

1. Solve $w^2 + 13w + 42 = 0$ by factoring.

2. Solve $v^2 - 8v - 33 = 0$ by factoring.

3. Mario is constructing a frame for a 10 in by 8 in photo. He wants the frame to be the same width all the way around and the total area of the frame and photo to be 120 square inches. What is the dimension of the frame?

4. Consider the function $f(x) = x^2 + 2x - 35$. If one of the zeros of the function is $x = -7$, then what is the other zero of the function?

5. Gabe drops a hammer from an apartment that is 30 meters above the ground. The height of the hammer from the ground (in meters), h, after t seconds is modeled by the function shown.

$$h(t) = -t^2 - t + 30$$

Find the number of seconds it will take for the hammer to hit the ground.

Ⓐ 0
Ⓑ 5
Ⓒ 10
Ⓓ 30

6. Fill in the missing portions of the function to rewrite $f(x) = 2x^2 + 14x + 24$ to reveal the zeros of the function. What are the zeros of $f(x)$?

Enter your answers in the boxes:

$g(x) = 2(x+ \boxed{})(x+ \boxed{})$

Zeros: $\boxed{}$ and $\boxed{}$

7. Which of the following quadratic equations has the solution set $\{-20, 9\}$?

☐ $x^2 - 9x + 20 = 0$
☐ $x^2 - 11x + 180 = 0$
☐ $x^2 + 11x - 180 = 0$
☐ $(x+20)(x-9) = 0$
☐ $(x-20)(x+9) = 0$
☐ $(x-5)(x-4) = 0$

Section 5 – Topic 4
Solving Other Quadratic Equations by Factoring

1. Solve for x: $2x^2 + 3x = 2$.

2. What are the solutions to $16x^2 - 12x = 54$? Select all that apply.

   ☐ $-\frac{9}{2}$ ☐ $\frac{3}{4}$

   ☐ $-\frac{9}{4}$ ☐ $\frac{3}{2}$

   ☐ $-\frac{3}{2}$ ☐ $\frac{9}{4}$

   ☐ $-\frac{3}{4}$

3. The area of a rooftop can be expressed as $9x^2 + 6x + 1$. The rooftop is a quadrilateral.

   Part A: What type of quadrilateral is the rooftop? Justify your answer.

   Part B: If the area of the rooftop is $361 \ m^2$, what is the length of one side of the rooftop?

4. The area of a rectangle is $12a^2 - a - 6$ square inches. The width is $4a - 3$ inches. What is the length?

   Ⓐ $(8a - 4)$ inches
   Ⓑ $(3a - 2)$ inches
   Ⓒ $(3a + 2)$ inches
   Ⓓ $(8a + 4)$ inches

5. A packing company is doing an inventory of boxes. Their most popular box is display below:

   Box dimensions: 2 ft., $(3x - 5)$ ft., $(2x - 1)$ ft.

   You can use the formula $V = lwh$ to find the volume of a box.

   The volume of the box is $40 \ ft^3$. What is the value of x? Find the length and the width of the box. Describe any extraneous solutions.

Section 5 – Topic 5
Solving Quadratic Equations by Factoring – Special Cases

1. Factor the expression $64f^2 - 225$.

2. Determine if $p^2 + 14p + 49$ is a perfect square trinomial. Justify your answer.

3. In the exit slip, Brady got everything wrong. He needed to factor $x^2 - 10x + 25$ and $16c^2 - 9$. This is his work.

$$x^2 - 10x + 25 = x^2 - 10x + 5^2$$
$$= x^2 - 2(x)(5) + 5^2$$
$$= (x + 5)(x - 5)$$

$$16c^2 - 9 = (4c)^2 - (3)^2$$
$$= (4c - 3)^2$$

Identify the error(s) in planning the solution or solving the problem. Write the correct solution.

4. A square painting has an area of $81x^2 - 90x + 25$. A second square painting has an area of $25x^2 + 30x + 9$.

    Part A: What is an expression that represents the difference of the areas of the paintings? Show two different ways to find the solution.

    Part B: The paintings have areas of $1{,}600\ in^2$ and $484\ in^2$, respectively. A potential buyer went to an exhibition and argued that the value of x for both paintings is the same. Is he right? Prove it.

5. The surface area of the box of cereal displayed below is $2x^2 + 48x + 88$.

What is the value of x if the box of cereal has an area of $192\ in^2$?

Section 5 – Topic 6
Solving Quadratic Equations by Taking Square Roots

1. Solve $x^2 - 81 = 0$.

2. Solve $2x^2 - 26 = 0$.

3. Which of the following are the roots of the quadratic function below? Select all that apply.

$$f(x) = x^2 - 144$$

☐ -72
☐ -12
☐ -2
☐ 0
☐ 2
☐ 12
☐ 72

4. Antoine is trying to find the roots for the quadratic function $f(x) = x^2 + 25$. He states that there is no solution. Is he correct? Justify your answer.

Practice Book - Section 5: Quadratic Equations and Functions - Part 1

5. Which quadratic function below has the largest positive solution? Explain your answer.

$f(x) = 2x^2 - 32$ $\qquad g(x) = 12x^2 - 48 \qquad$ $h(x) = 100x^2$

6. Manny is repairing a window air conditioning unit on the 11th floor of a building and is approximately 98 feet off the ground. While working, Manny drops his screwdriver. The height h of the screwdriver in feet after t seconds of falling from the 11th floor is modeled by the function $h = -16t^2 + 98$. How long will it take for the screwdriver to reach the ground? Show your work below and round to the nearest tenth if necessary.

7. What is the value of c so that -9 and 9 are both solutions of $x^2 + c = 103$?

Section 5 – Topic 7
Solving Quadratic Equations by Completing the Square

1. Use the quadratic equation $x^2 + 18x = 25$ to answer the following questions.

   Part A: Find the value of c that will result in a perfect square trinomial.
   $$x^2 + 18x + c = 25 + c$$

   Part B: Rewrite the above equation into a perfect square binomial form.
   $$(x + \underline{})^2 = \underline{}$$

   Part C: What is the value of x?

2. Find the roots of the quadratic function by completing the square:
   $x^2 + 4x - 1 = 0$.

3. The rectangular poster shown at the right measures $2w - 30$ by w. The poster has an area of $5400 \, cm^2$. What is the value of w?

4. The area of a rectangular television screen is $1837 \, in^2$. The width of the screen is 22.4 inches longer than the height. Therefore, the quadratic equation that can be used to represent the area of the television screen is $h(h + 22.4) = 1837$. If you multiply, you then have the equivalent equation, $h^2 + 22.4h = 1837$. Complete the square to find the dimensions of the screen.

5. The area of a rectangular television screen is $3456 \, in^2$. The width of the screen is 24 inches longer than the height. What is a quadratic equation that represents the area of the screen? What are the dimensions of the screen?

   Part A: What is the quadratic equation that represents the area of the television screen?

   Part B: What are the dimensions of the screen?

Section 5 – Topic 8
Deriving the Quadratic Formula

1. In the left column, fill in the missing steps of the derivation of the quadratic formula. In the right column, explain the process taken to arrive at that step. The first two rows have been completed for you.

Step	Explanation
$ax^2 + bx + c = 0$	The quadratic equation is set equal to 0 to solve for x-intercepts.
$x^2 + \dfrac{b}{a}x + \dfrac{c}{a} = 0$	In order for the leading coefficient to equal 1, we must divide every term by "a".
$x^2 + \dfrac{b}{a}x + \dfrac{b^2}{4a^2} = -\dfrac{c}{a} + \dfrac{b^2}{4a^2}$	
$\sqrt{(x + \dfrac{b}{2a})^2} = \sqrt{\dfrac{b^2 - 4ac}{4a^2}}$	
$x = -\dfrac{b}{2a} \pm \dfrac{\sqrt{b^2 - 4ac}}{2a}$	
	Fractions with common denominators can be rewritten as one fraction. This results in the quadratic formula.

Practice Book - Section 5: Quadratic Equations and Functions - Part 1

Section 5 – Topic 9
Solving Quadratic Equations Using the Quadratic Formula

1. A rocket carrying fireworks is launched from a hill 80 feet above a lake. The rocket will fall into the lake after exploding at its maximum height. The rocket's height above the surface of the lake is represented by $h = -16t^2 + 64t + 80$. How many seconds after the rocket launched will it hit the lake?

   Define your terms:

   $a =$ [   ] $b =$ [   ] $c =$ [   ]

   Now, set up the quadratic formula:

   $$x = \frac{-() \pm \sqrt{()^2 - 4()()}}{2()}$$

   Part A: Find the solutions to the quadratic formula.

   Part B: Which solution is the correct solution for this scenario? Justify your answer.

2. A rock is thrown from the top of a tall building. The distance, in feet, between the rock and the ground t seconds after it is thrown is represented by $d = -16t^2 - 4t + 382$. How long after the rock is thrown is it 370 feet from the ground?

3. If the measure of one side of a square is increased by 2 centimeters and the measure of the adjacent side is decreased by 2 centimeters, the area of the resulting rectangle is 32 square centimeters. Find the measure of one side of the square.

4. Joe's rectangular garden is 6 meters long and 4 meters wide. He wishes to double the area of his garden by increasing its length and width by the same amount. Find the number of meters by which each dimension must be increased.

5. After t seconds, a ball tossed in the air from the ground level reaches a height of h feet given by the equation $h = 144t - 16t^2$. After how many seconds will the ball hit the ground before rebounding?

Section 5 – Topic 10
Quadratic Functions in Action

1. The function $M(x) = 5x^2 - 160x + 6179$ models the number of miles, in millions, US passengers travel on a train for the period of 1970 to 2000, where x is the number of years since 1970.

   Part A: Which equivalent form reveals the minimum number of miles, in millions, US passengers traveled on a train for the period of 1970 to 2000?

   Ⓐ $M(x) = 5x(x - 32) + 6179$
   Ⓑ $M(x) = 5(x - 16)^2 + 4899$
   Ⓒ $M(x) = 5(x - 32)^2 + 1059$
   Ⓓ $M(x) = 5(x - 16)^2 + 6435$

   Part B: According to the model, in
   - 1986
   - 2002
   - 2016
   - 2032

   the number of miles US passengers traveled on a train reached a minimum of _____ million miles.
   - 1,059
   - 4,899
   - 6,179
   - 6,435

2. King James Factory provides farms and restaurants across the nation with corn syrup. The figure below shows the profit function for the King James Factory with the relative maximum labeled.

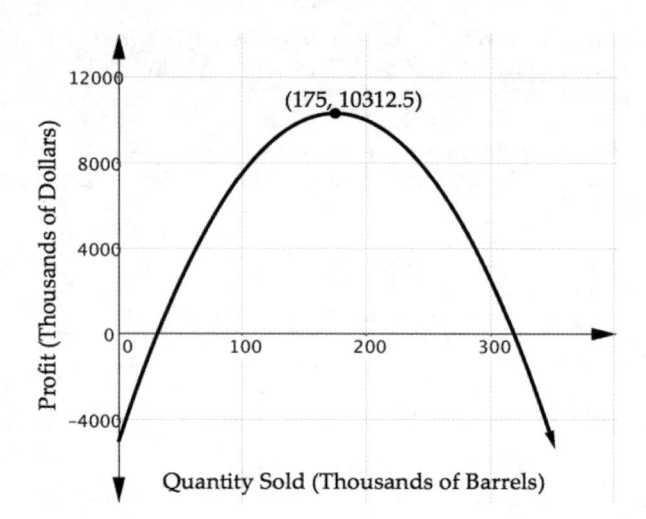

[Graph showing a downward-opening parabola with vertex at (175, 10312.5). X-axis labeled "Quantity Sold (Thousands of Barrels)" with values 0, 100, 200, 300. Y-axis labeled "Profit (Thousands of Dollars)" with values -4000, 0, 4000, 8000, 12000.]

Part A: How many barrels of corn syrup do you recommend that King James Factory produce, assuming that they will sell everything that is produced? Why?

Part B: When will King James Factory lose money? Justify your answer.

Part C: When will King James Factory break even, that it will neither make a profit nor lose money? Justify your answer.

3. The function $C(x) = -2x^2 + 38x + 40$ models the sales, in hundreds of millions of dollars, of compact discs for years since 1990.

Part A: Rewrite the function to reveal when sales of compact discs are $0.

Part B: What are the zeros of the function?

Part C: Use the context to interpret the zeros.

4. Engineers are designing a rollercoaster that at one point goes underground. The rollercoaster's path underground is a large curve. The engineers use the function shown to model the elevation, E, in feet and t, time, in seconds, of the rollercoaster's path while it is underground.

$$E(t) = t^2 - 10t + 16$$

Part A: Write an equivalent form of $E(t)$ that can be used to find the time when the rollercoaster goes underground and the time the rollercoaster returns above ground.

$E(t) = $ _____

Part B: How long, in seconds, was the rollercoaster underground?

5. A scientist is performing a study on mosquitoes. She collects water with mosquito larvae and places it in an enclosed container in her lab. The scientist uses the data from the study to create the function, $M(t) = -3t^2 + 57t - 144$, where t is the number of days in the study.

Part A: Which equivalent form of $M(t)$ reveals when the mosquitoes first appeared in the container and when there were no more mosquitoes in the container?

- Ⓐ $M(t) = -3(t - 16)(t - 3)$
- Ⓑ $M(t) = -3(t - 19)^2 + 217$
- Ⓒ $M(t) = -3t(t - 48)$
- Ⓓ $M(t) = -3t(t - 19) - 144$

Part B: How long were there mosquitoes in the container?

- Ⓐ 13 days
- Ⓑ 16 days
- Ⓒ 19 days
- Ⓓ 48 days

6. Rosa has a rectangular shaped backyard where the length is two less than twice the width. If the area of the garden is 420 square feet, find the dimensions of Rosa's garden

Section 6: Quadratic Equations and Functions – Part 2
Student Learning Plan

Topic Number	Topic Name	Date Completed	Study Expert(s)	Check Your Understanding Score
1	Observations from a Graph of a Quadratic Function			
2	Nature of the Zeros of Quadratic Equations and Functions			
3	Graphing Quadratic Functions Using a Table			
4	Graphing Quadratic Functions Using the Vertex and Intercepts			
5	Graphing Quadratic Functions Using Vertex Form – Part 1			
6	Graphing Quadratic Functions Using Vertex Form – Part 2			
7	Transformations of the Dependent Variable of Quadratic Functions			
8	Transformations of the Independent Variable of Quadratic Functions			
9	Finding Solution Sets to Systems of Equations Using Tables of Values and Successive Approximations			
Honors 1	Systems of Equations with Quadratic Equations			

*Honors resources are available online.

What did you learn in this section? What questions do you still have?

Who was your favorite Study Expert for this section? Why?

Section 6 – Topic 1
Observations from a Graph of a Quadratic Function

1. The point $(4, -2)$ is the vertex of the graph of a quadratic function. The points $(8, 6)$ and $(2, 0)$ also fall on the graph of the function. Complete the graph of this quadratic function by first finding two additional points on the graph.

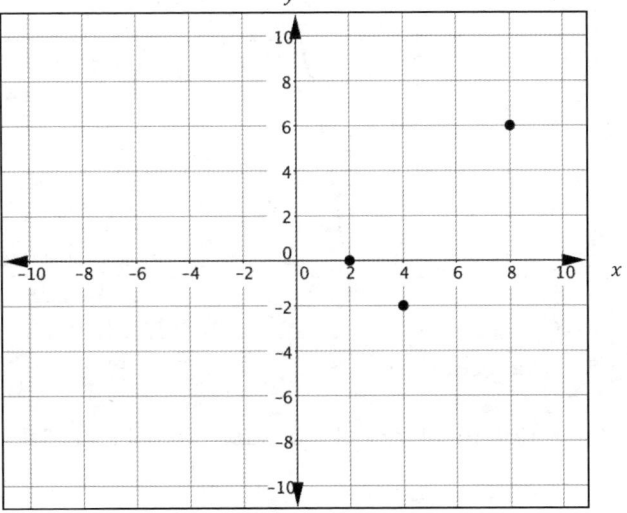

   Part A: What is the y-intercept of the graph?

   Part B: What are the x-intercepts?

   Part C: Find the interval on which the rate of change is always positive.

   Part D: What is the sign of the leading coefficient for this quadratic function? How do you know?

2. Toy Universe is manufacturing a new toy and deciding on a price that will result in a maximum profit. The graph below represents profit P generated by each price of a toy x.

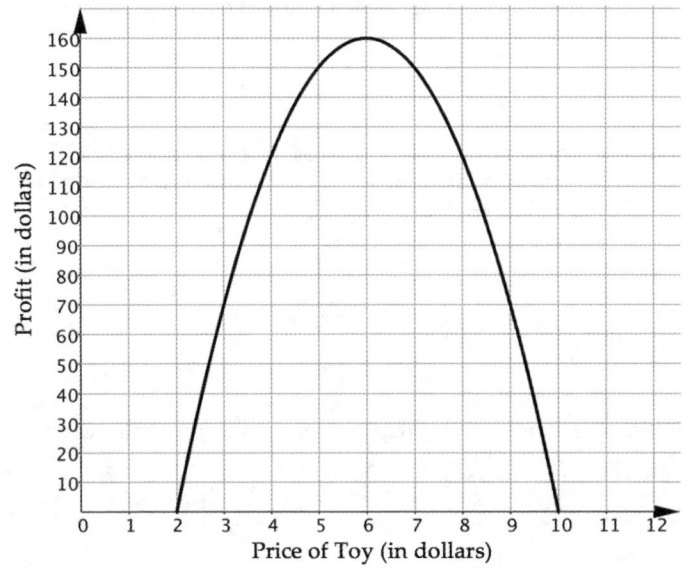

   Part A: If the company wants to make a maximum profit, what should the price of a new toy be?

   Part B: What is the minimum price of a toy that will produce profit for the company? Explain your answer.

   Part C: Estimate the value of $P(10)$ and explain what the value means in the problem and how this may be possible.

   Part D: If the company wants to make a profit of $137, for how much should the toy be sold?

Practice Book - Section 6: Quadratic Equations and Functions - Part 2

91

Part E: Find the domain that will only result in a profit for the company and find its corresponding range of profit.

Part F: The company owner believes that selling the toy at a higher price will result in a greater profit. Explain to the owner how selling the toy at a higher price will affect the profit.

3. Write the equation for this graph in the space provided on the graph.

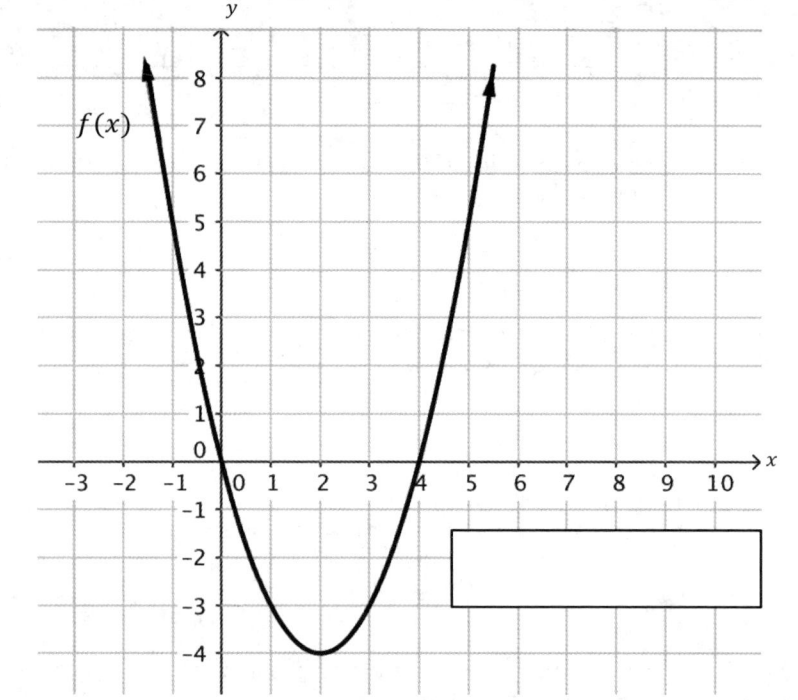

4. The graph of a quadratic function in shown below.

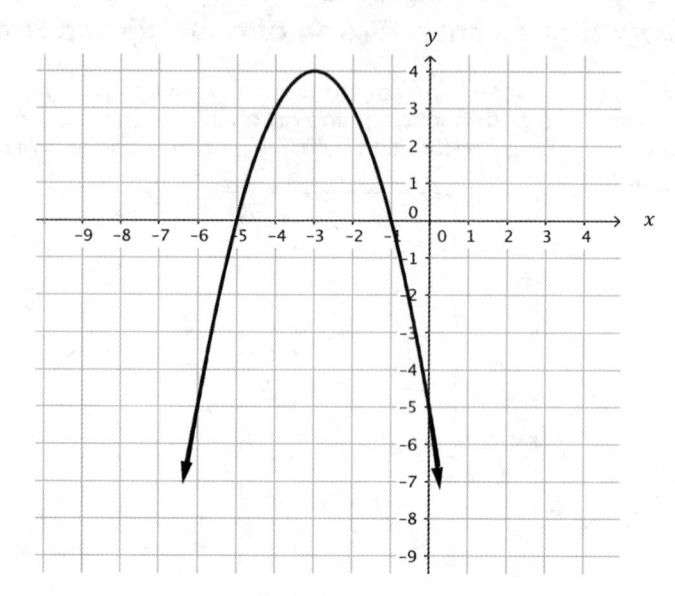

Which statements about this graph are **not** true? Select **all** that apply.

☐ The graph has a y-intercept at $(0, 5)$.
☐ The graph has a relative maximum point $(-3, 4)$.
☐ The graph has an x-intercept at $(1, 0)$.
☐ The graph has the y-axis as a line of symmetry.
☐ The graph has zeros at $x = -5$ and $x = -1$.
☐ The graph represents the function $f(x) = -x^2 - 6x - 5$.

5. Consider functions $f(x)$ and $g(x)$ graphed below.

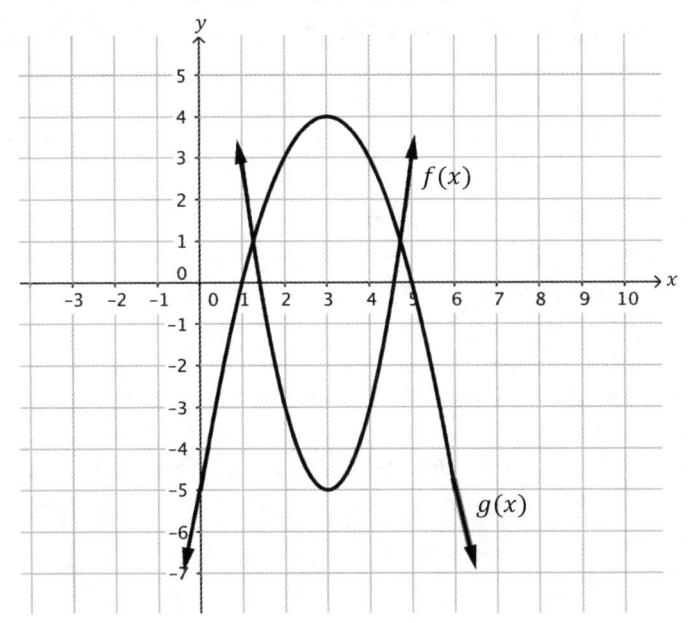

Which of the following statements are true about $f(x)$ and $g(x)$?

☐ The graphs share the same axis of symmetry.
☐ The y-intercept for $f(x)$ is greater than the y-intercept for $g(x)$.
☐ $f(2) + g(4) = 0$
☐ $f(-4) < g(0)$
☐ The domain of $f(x)$ has more elements than the domain of $g(x)$.
☐ The graphs share the same relative maximum.

Section 6 – Topic 2
Nature of the Zeros of Quadratic Equations and Functions

1. Use the discriminant to determine if the following quadratic equations have complex or real solution(s). If an equation has real solution(s), determine the solution(s).

Part A: $4x^2 - 3x - 10 = 0$

Part B: $x^2 - 14x + 49 = 0$

Part C: $g(x) = x^2 - 8x - 20$

Part D: $h(x) = x^2 - 9x + 36$

Part E: $3(x + 2)^2 + 26 = 0$

2. Create three quadratic equations that have complex solutions. Justify your answer.

3. Create three quadratic equations that have one real solution.

4. Which of the following quadratic equations have two real solutions? Select all that apply.

☐ $9x^2 - 12x + 4 = 0$
☐ $-x^2 = 4 - 5x$
☐ $2x^2 - 8x = 24$
☐ $5x^2 - 10x = 3$
☐ $x^2 - 2x = -5$

5. Explain the difference between quadratic equations with one solution, two solutions, and complex solutions.

Section 6 – Topic 3
Graphing Quadratic Functions Using a Table

1. A model rocket was launched from a podium 5 meters above ground at an initial velocity of $98 \ m/s$. The function that models height (in meters) with respect to time (in seconds) is $h(t) = 5 + 98t - 4.9t^2$.

   Part A: Complete the table below.

Time (seconds)	0	5	10	15	20
Elevation (meters)					

   Part B: Graph function $h(t)$ on the following coordinate grid.

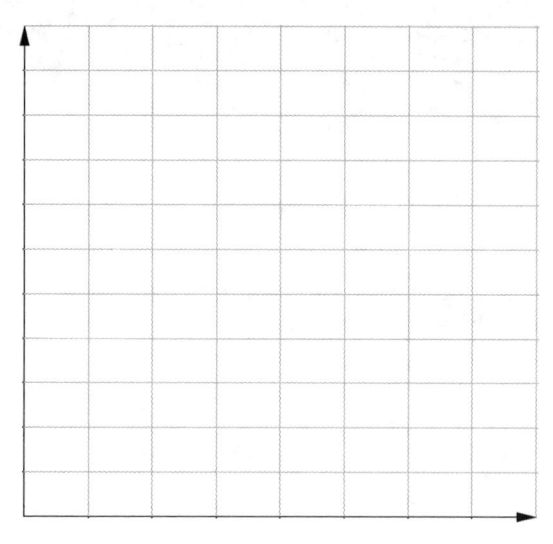

   Part C: Estimate the time when the model rocket lands on the ground. Justify your answer.

2. Consider the following table of values.

x	−1	0	2	4	5
$f(x)$	8	3	−1	3	8

Which of the following is the graph corresponding to the table of values?

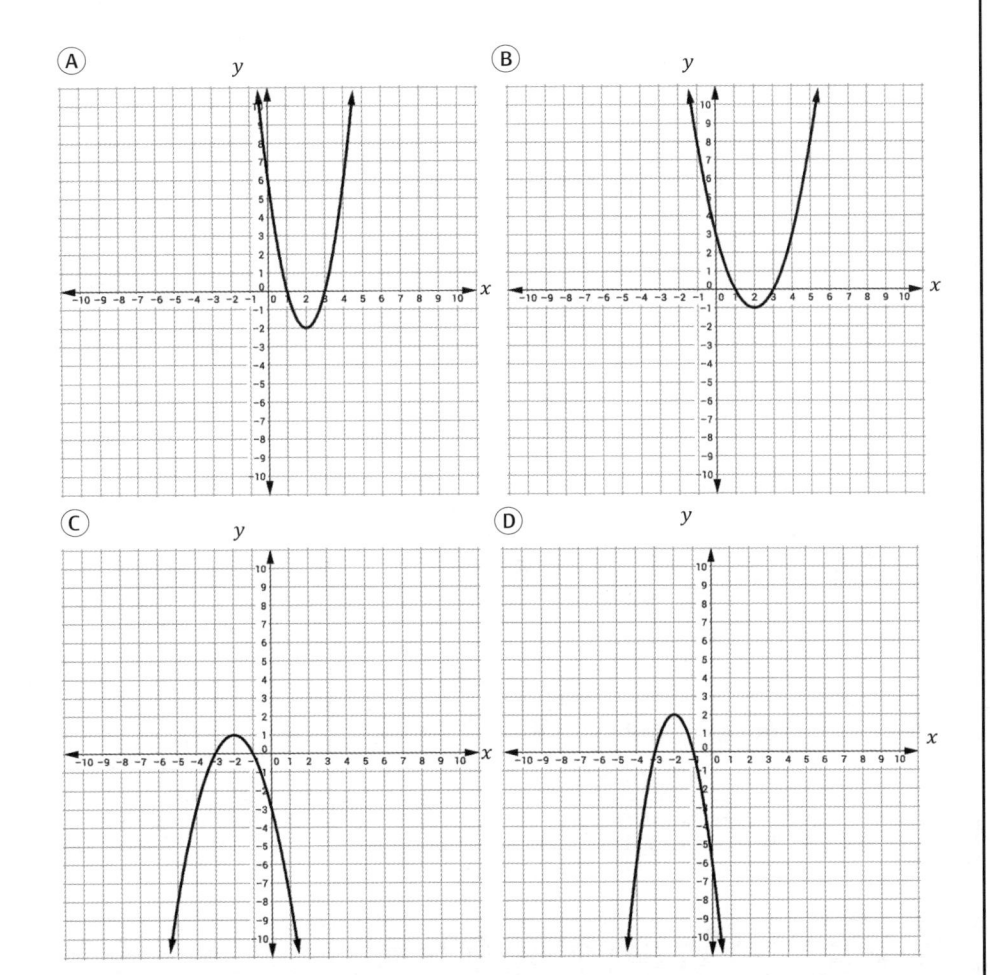

A)

B)

C)

D)

3. The average rainfall of a certain geographical location is modeled by the table below.

Part A: Plot the data on the graph below if January is equivalent to $x = 0$.

Month	Rainfall (in inches)
Jan	72
Feb	75.7
Mar	78.7
Apr	81
May	82.6
Jun	83.6
Jul	84
Aug	83.6
Sep	82.7
Oct	81
Nov	78.6
Dec	75.7

Part B: What type of geographical location might be represented by this graph?

Practice Book - Section 6: Quadratic Equations and Functions - Part 2

4. Pierre was plotting the quadratic function $f(x) = -x^2 + 8x$ for an exit ticket. His work is shown below.

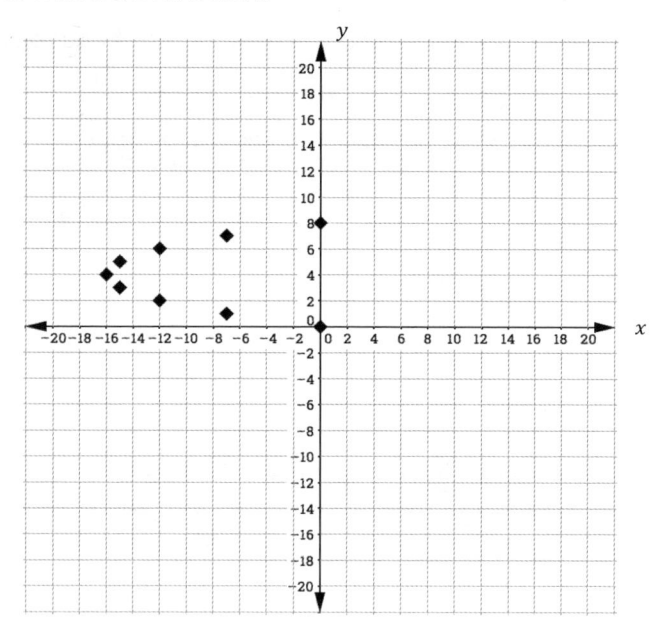

Part A: Complete the table below and graph the function on the same coordinate system above.

x	$f(x)$
0	
1	
2	
3	
4	

x	$f(x)$
5	
6	
7	
8	

Part B: His teacher marked it incorrect. Explain why Pierre's work was counted incorrect.

Section 6 – Topic 4
Graphing Quadratic Functions Using the Vertex and Intercepts

1. Jessica is eating a bag of Sour Skittles. Her friend asks her to share, and Jessica throws over an extra bag. Her friend does not catch the bag, and it hits the ground. The distance from the ground (height) for the bag of candies is modeled by the function $h(t) = -16t^2 + 32t + 4$, where $h(t)$ is the height (distance from the ground in feet) of the candies and t is the number of seconds the candies are in the air. Describe in a paragraph what the graph of this scenario would look like.

2. Graph the following function and identify the key features of the graph.

$$g(x) = -2(x-1)(x+5)$$

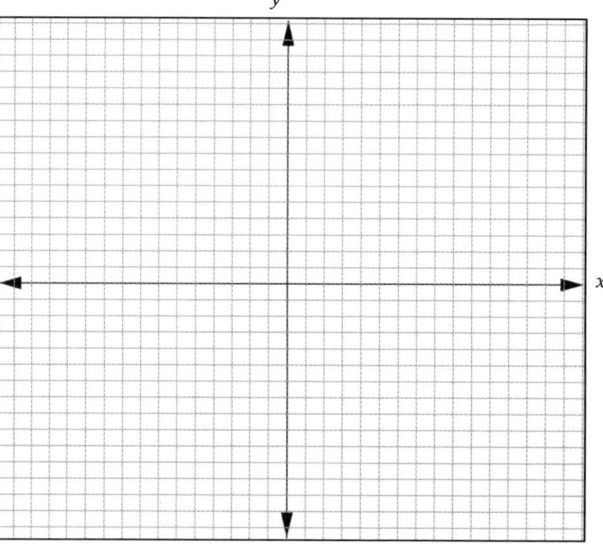

96

Practice Book - Section 6: Quadratic Equations and Functions - Part 2

3. Graph the following function, $h(x) = x^2 + 7x + 6$, using the coordinate grid below. Identify the key features of the graph, including the x–intercepts, y–intercept, axis of symmetry, and vertex.

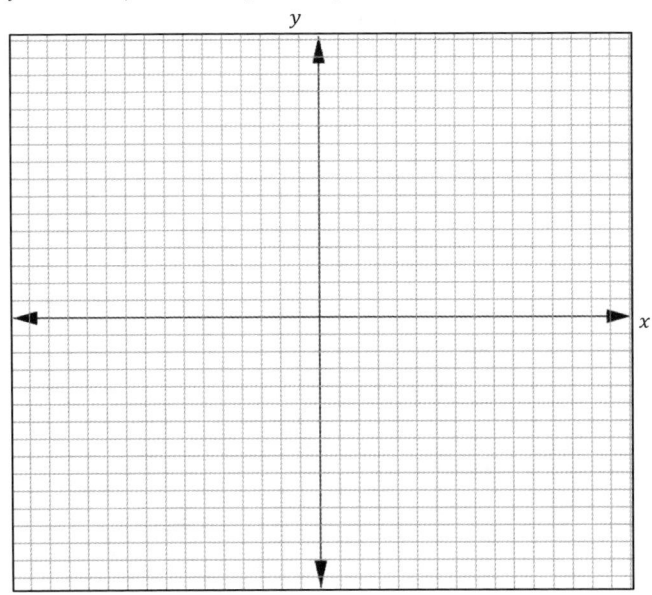

4. Write a short "real-world" story about this graph using the key features of a graph of a quadratic equation.

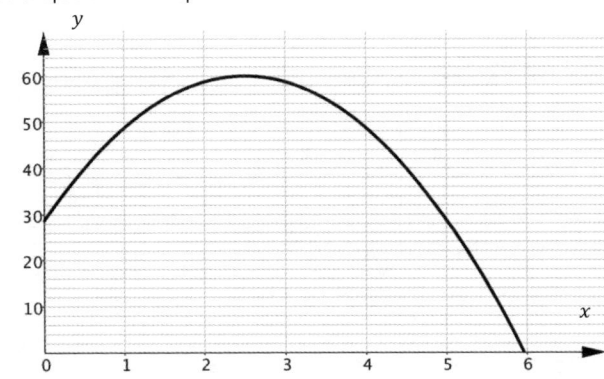

5. In a physics lab, an artifact is dropped from the roof of the school building, 98 feet above the ground. The height h (in feet) of the ball above the ground is given by the function $h(t) = -16t^2 + 98$, where t is the time in seconds.

   Part A: Graph the function.

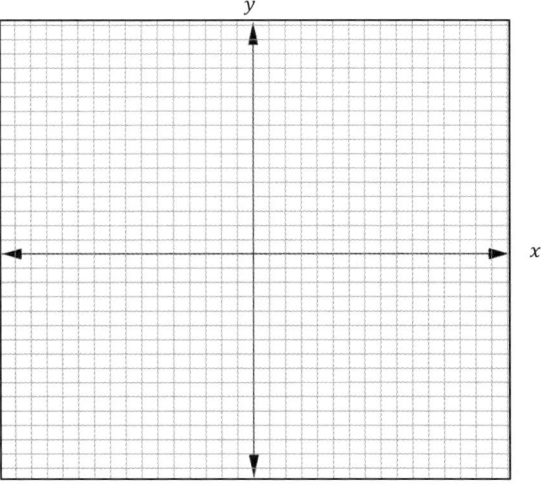

   Part B: How far has the artifact fallen from time $t = 0$ to $t = 1$?

   Part C: Does the artifact fall the same distance from time $t = 1$ to time $t = 2$ as it does from $t = 0$ to $t = 1$? Explain.

Practice Book - Section 6: Quadratic Equations and Functions - Part 2

6. *MobiStar* is a mobile services company that sells 800 phones each week when it charges $80 per phone. It sells 40 more phones per week for each $2 decrease in price. The company's revenue is the product of the number of phones sold and the price of each phone. What price should the company charge to maximize its revenue?

Part A: Let d represent the number of $2 decreases in price. Let r be the company's revenue. Write a quadratic function that reflects the company's revenue.

Hint: The number of phones sold will be $800 + 40d$ since they sell 40 more phones for every $2 decrease. The price for the phones will be $80 - 2d$ since d is the number of decreases and each decrease is $2.

Part B: Find the vertex of the quadratic function above. How will finding the vertex help you determine at what price the company should charge to maximize its revenue?

Part C: Graph this function and show in the graph what price the company should charge.

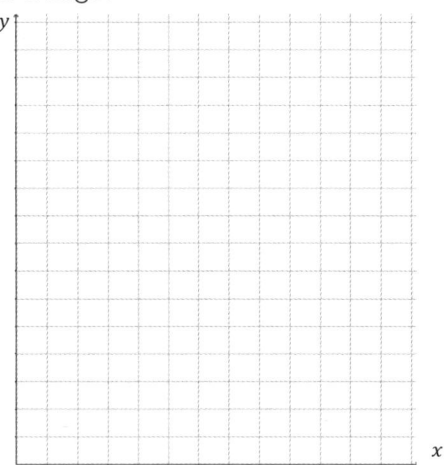

Section 6 – Topic 5
Graphing Quadratic Functions Using Vertex Form – Part 1

1. Identify the vertex, complete the table, and graph $g(x) = (x - 4)^2 - 5$.

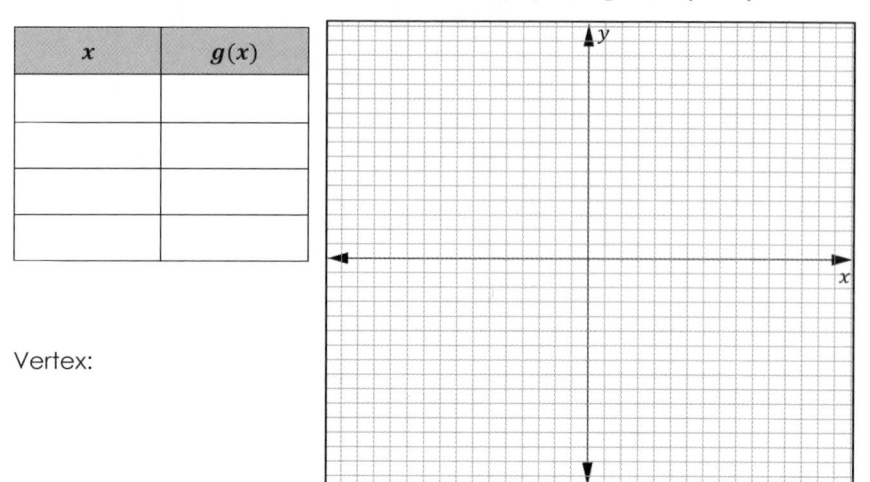

x	$g(x)$

Vertex:

2. Identify the vertex, complete the table, and graph $h(x) = (x + 1)^2 + 4$.

x	$h(x)$

Vertex:

3. Students in Mr. Mackie's art class went outside to draw a rainbow, which follows a parabolic path and has the equation of $y = -0.1(x-1)^2 + 6$, where x and y are measured in centimeters. Graph the function.

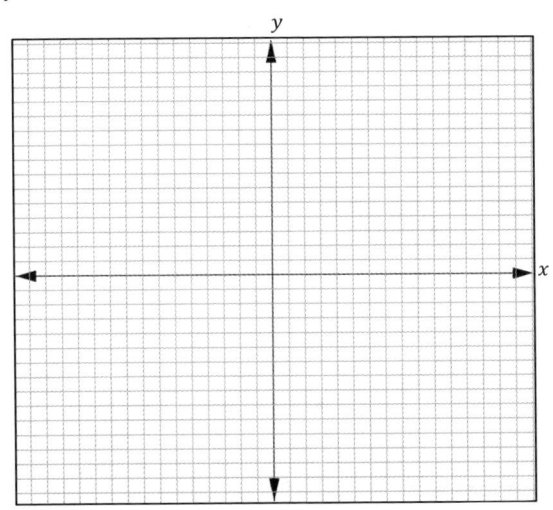

If the height of the rainbow is 6 cm, how far away are the end points of the rainbow from one another?

4. Select and circle the graph that corresponds to this equation $y = 3(x-2)^2 - 2$.

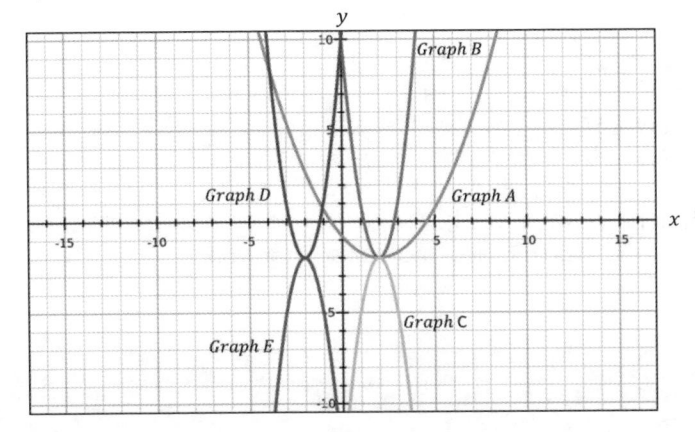

5. Toretto and O'Conner graphed two different quadratic functions in vertex form. Toretto graphed $f(x) = (x+3)^2 + 1$ and O'Conner graphed $g(x) = -(x-3)^2 + 1$. Both of them drew the same graph.

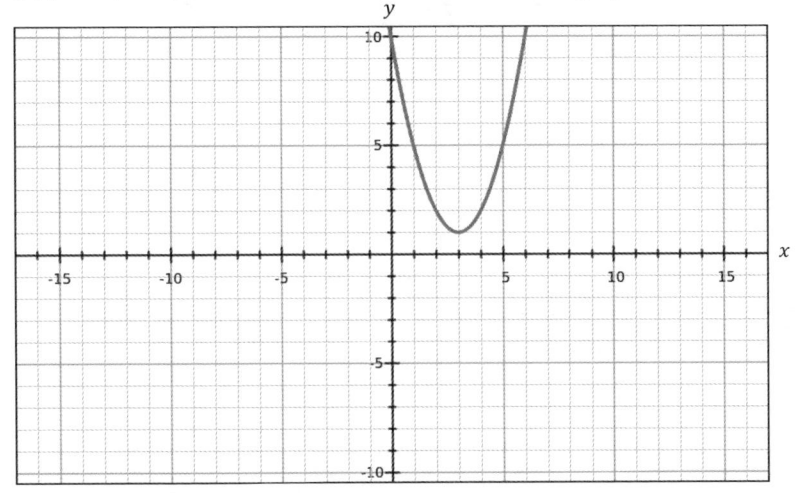

Part A: Who drew the correct graph?

Ⓐ Both of them are correct because the functions are the same.

Ⓑ Neither of them is correct because their graph either has the wrong vertex or the wrong direction.

Ⓒ O'Conner is correct because the vertex is $(3, 1)$.

Ⓓ Toretto is correct because the graph is positive.

Part B: Justify your answer.

Section 6 – Topic 6
Graphing Quadratic Functions Using Vertex Form – Part 2

1. Write $f(x) = x^2 - 6x + 8$ in vertex form, using decimals if necessary.

   Identify the vertex, fill in the table, and graph $f(x)$.

x	$f(x)$

   Vertex:

2. For the function $m(x) = 3x^2 + 13x - 30$, determine the key features.

3. Write $g(x) = 8x^2 - 14x + 3$ in vertex form, using decimals if necessary.

   Identify the vertex, fill in the table, and graph $g(x)$.

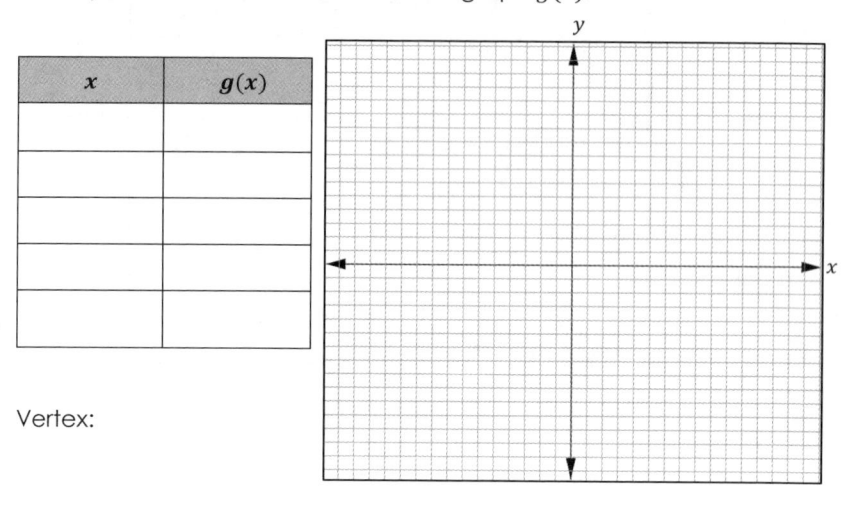

x	$g(x)$

   Vertex:

4. April rewrote a quadratic function in vertex form.

   $h(x) = 5x^2 - 30x + 30$

   Step 1: $h(x) = 5(x^2 - 6x + \quad) + 30$
   Step 2: $h(x) = 5(x^2 - 6x + 9) + 30 - 45$
   Step 3: $h(x) = 5(x - 3)^2 + 15$

   April said that the vertex is $(3, 15)$. Is April correct? If not, identify the step in which April made the mistake and correct her work.

Section 6 – Topic 7
Transformations of the Dependent Variable of Quadratic Functions

1. Consider the following standard.

   > Identify the effect on the graph of replacing $f(x)$ by $f(x) + k$, $kf(x)$, $f(kx)$, and $f(x + k)$ for specific values of k (both positive and negative); find the value of k given the graphs.

   Part A: Circle the parts of the standard that indicate a transformation on the dependent variable.

   Part B: Describe the transformations.

2. Consider the following functions.

   $$f(x) = x^2 + 1$$
   $$g(x) = f(x) + 3$$
   $$h(x) = f(x) - 3$$

   Part A: Complete the following table for the functions.

x	$f(x)$	$g(x)$	$h(x)$
-2			
-1			
0			
1			
2			

   Part B: Graph the functions on the same coordinate plane.

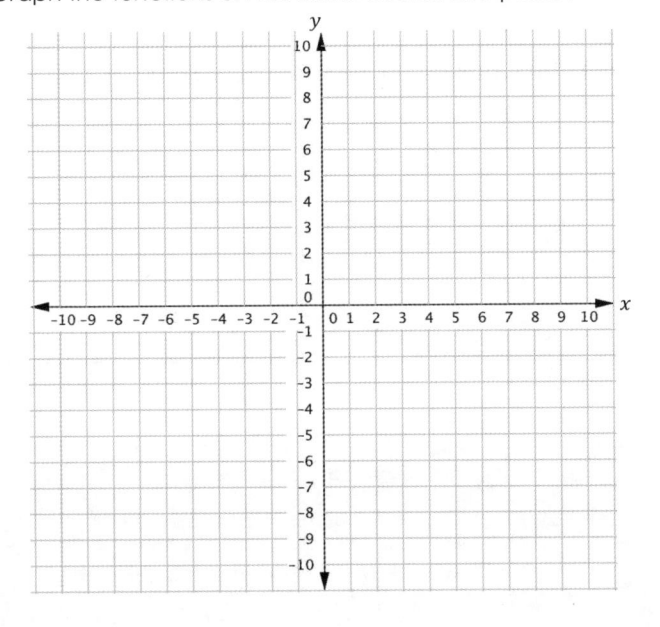

3. Consider the following functions.

$$f(x) = x^2 + 1$$
$$g(x) = -f(x)$$
$$h(x) = 2f(x)$$
$$j(x) = \frac{1}{2}f(x)$$

Part A: Complete the following table for the functions.

x	$f(x)$	$g(x)$	$h(x)$	$j(x)$
-2				
-1				
0				
1				
2				

Part B: Graph the functions on the same coordinate plane.

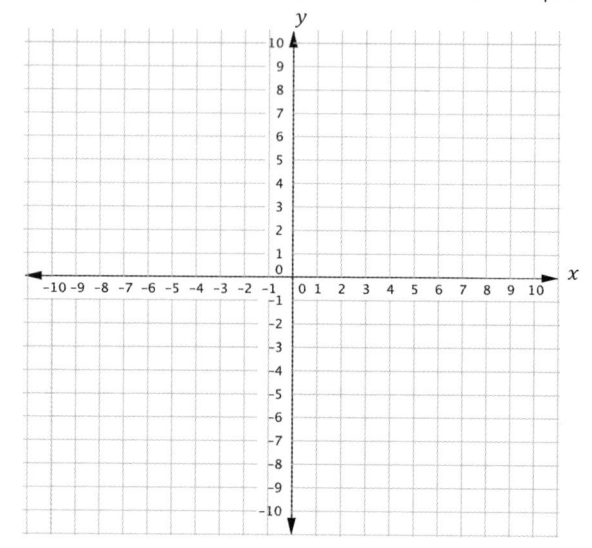

4. Consider the function $f(x) = x^2 + 2x + 1$.

Part A: Write a function that shifts $f(x)$ up 5 units.

Part B: Write a function that shifts $f(x)$ down 8 units.

Part C: Write a function that vertically compresses $f(x)$ by $\frac{1}{4}$ units.

Part D: Write a function that vertically stretches $f(x)$ by 6 units.

Part E: Write a function that reflects $f(x)$ about the x-axis.

Section 6 – Topic 8
Transformations of the Independent Variable of Quadratic Functions

1. Consider the following standard.

   > Identify the effect on the graph of replacing $f(x)$ by $f(x) + k$, $kf(x)$, $f(kx)$, and $f(x + k)$ for specific values of k (both positive and negative); find the value of k given the graphs.

   Part A: Circle the parts of the standard that indicate a transformation on the independent variable.

   Part B: Describe the transformations.

2. Consider the following functions.

$$f(x) = x^2 + 1$$
$$g(x) = f(x - 5)$$
$$h(x) = f(x + 3)$$

   Part A: Complete the following table for the functions.

x	$f(x)$	x	$g(x)$	x	$h(x)$
-2					
-1					
0					
1					
2					

   Part B: Graph the functions on the same coordinate plane.

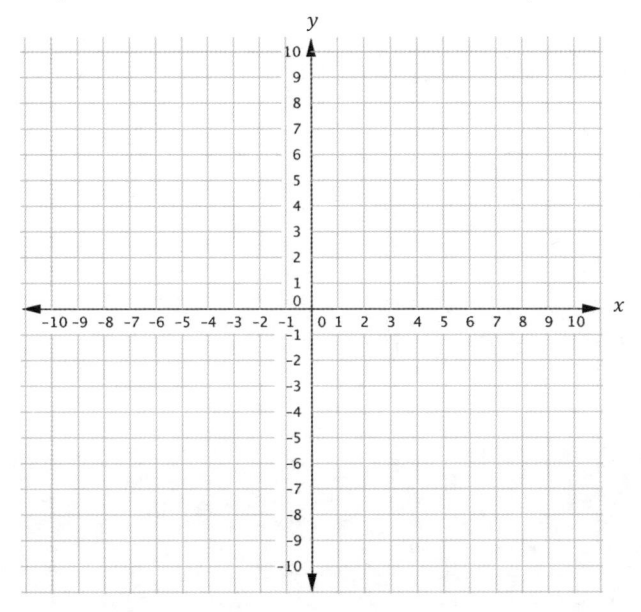

3. Consider the following functions.

$$f(x) = x^2 + 1$$

$$g(x) = f\left(\frac{1}{2}x\right)$$

$$h(x) = f(4x)$$

Part A: Complete the following table for the functions.

x	$f(x)$	x	$g(x)$	x	$h(x)$
−2					
−1					
0					
1					
2					

Part B: Graph the functions on the same coordinate plane.

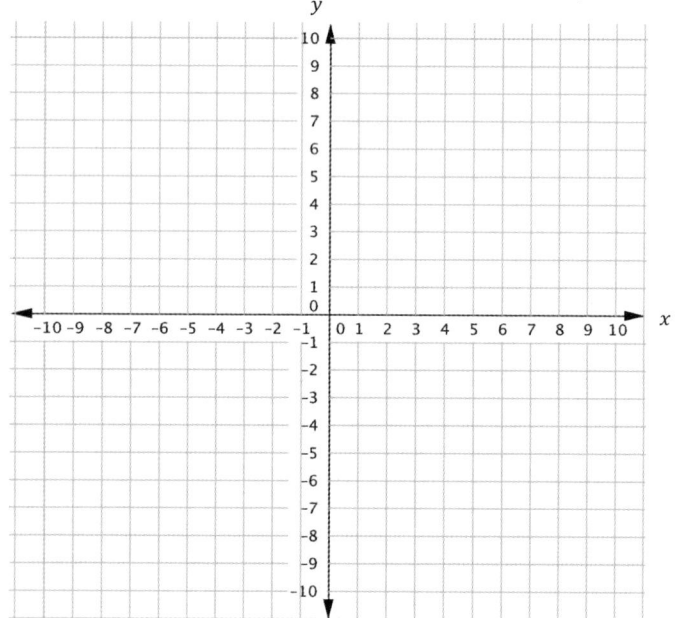

4. Consider the function $f(x) = x^2 - 4$.

Part A: Write a function that shifts $f(x)$ left 5 units.

Part B: Write a function that shifts $f(x)$ right 8 units.

Part C: Write a function that horizontally stretches $f(x)$ by $\frac{1}{4}$ units.

Part D: Write a function that horizontally compresses $f(x)$ by 6 units.

Section 6 – Topic 9
Finding Solution Sets to Systems of Equations Using Tables of Values and Successive Approximations

1. Use the graphs to verify the solutions of the systems of equations.

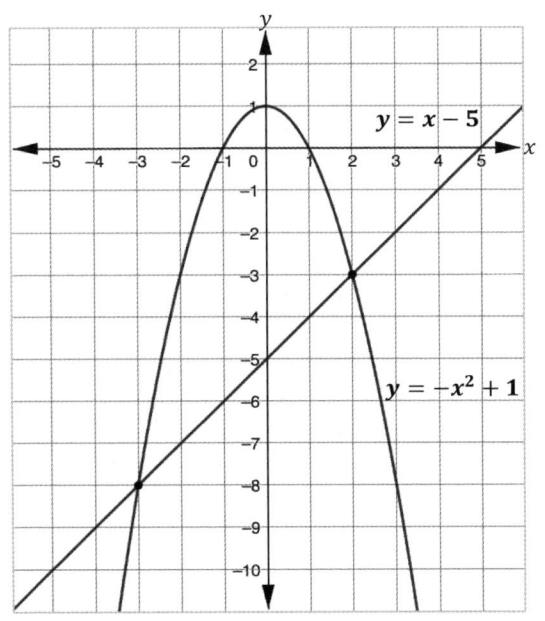

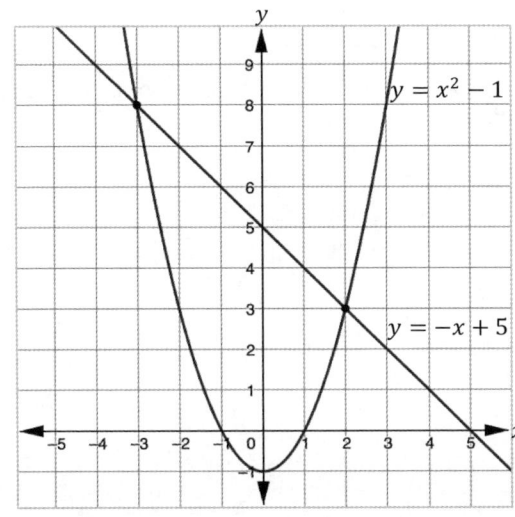

   $y = x - 5$
   $y = -x^2 + 1$

   $y = x^2 - 1$
   $y = -x + 5$

2. Consider the following functions.

   $f(x) = x + 3$
   $g(x) = -3(x - 1)$

   Part A: Complete the table of values for the functions.

x	$f(x)$	$g(x)$
-3		
-2		
-1		
0		
1		
2		
3		

   Part B: Use the table to determine the solution(s) to the system of equations.

Practice Book - Section 6: Quadratic Equations and Functions - Part 2

3. Consider the following functions.

$$f(x) = x^2 + 3$$
$$g(x) = 7x - 7$$

Part A: Complete the table of values for the functions.

x	$f(x)$	$g(x)$
0		
1		
2		
3		
4		
5		
6		
7		

Part B: Use the table to determine the solution(s) to the system of equations.

4. Consider the following functions.

$$f(x) = \sqrt{x+4}$$
$$g(x) = \frac{x-2}{5}$$

Part A: Complete the table of values for the functions.

x	$f(x)$	$g(x)$
−4		
−3		
0		
5		
12		
21		
32		
45		

Part B: Use the table to determine the solution(s) to the system of equations.

5. Use the process of successive approximations to find the positive x solution of the system to the nearest tenth.

$$g(x) = x^2 + 13$$
$$h(x) = 3x + 14$$

x	$g(x)$	$h(x)$
0	13	14
1	14	17
2	17	20
3	22	23
4	29	26

6. Consider the following functions.

$$g(x) = x^2 + 3$$
$$h(x) = 2x + 5$$

Part A: Complete the table of values for the functions.

x	$g(x)$	$h(x)$
-2		
-1		
0		
1		
2		
3		
4		

Part B: Use the process of successive approximations to find the positive x solution of the system to the nearest tenth.

Section 7: Exponential Functions
Student Learning Plan

Topic Number	Topic Name	Date Completed	Study Expert(s)	Check Your Understanding Score
1	Geometric Sequences			
2	Exponential Functions			
3	Graphs of Exponential Functions – Part 1			
4	Graphs of Exponential Functions – Part 2			
5	Growth and Decay Rates of Exponential Functions			
6	Transformations of Exponential Functions			
Honors 1	Geometric Series			

*Honors resources are available online.

What did you learn in this section? What questions do you still have?

Who was your favorite Study Expert for this section? Why?

Section 7 – Topic 1
Geometric Sequences

1. Consider the sequence 7, 21, 63, 189, 567 ...

    Part A: In the statement below, circle the correct word in each of the shaded segments to describe the sequence above.

    This is an example of a(n) arithmetic | **geometric** sequence. Each term in the sequence is the product of the **previous** | first term and a real number r.

    Part B: Complete the tables below using a recursive process to describe the sequence above.

Term Number	Sequence Term	Term
1	a_1	7
2	a_2	$21 = 7 \cdot 3$
3	a_3	
4	a_4	
5	a_5	$567 = 189 \cdot 3$
6	a_6	

Function Notation	
$A(1)$	a_1
$A(2)$	$3a_1$
$A(3)$	$3a_2$
	$3a_3$
$A(5)$	
$A(6)$	

    Part C: Write a recursive formula that we could use to find any term in the sequence.

    Part D: What is the 9th term in the sequence?

    Part E: Complete the tables below using an explicit process to describe the sequence 7, 21, 63, 189, 567 ...

Term Number	Sequence Term	Term
1	a_1	7
2	a_2	$21 = 7 \cdot 3$
3	a_3	
4	a_4	$189 = 7 \cdot 3 \cdot 3 \cdot 3$
5	a_5	
6	a_6	

Function Notation	
$A(1)$	a_1
$A(2)$	$3a_1$
$A(3)$	$3^2 a_1$
$A(4)$	
$A(5)$	$3^4 a_1$
$A(6)$	

Practice Book - Section 7: Exponential Functions

Part F: Write an explicit formula that we could use to find any term in the sequence.

Part G: What is the 14th term in the sequence?

2. Consider the following statement and circle the correct word in each of the shaded segments of the statement.

   The recursive process uses the first | previous term, whereas the explicit process uses the first | previous term.

3. Sketch the graph of the geometric sequence found in the table.

Term Number	Term
1	2
2	4
3	8
4	16
5	32
6	64

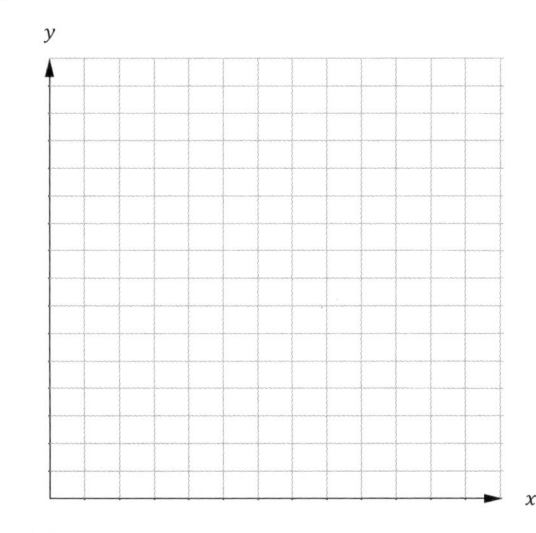

4. Consider the sequence 3, −9, 27, −81, …

   Part A: Write an explicit formula for the sequence.

   Part B: Write a recursive formula for the sequence.

   Part C: Find the 14th term of the sequence.

5. Explain why geometric sequences are exponential functions.

6. When expressing an exponential function as a recursive function, it is important to remember that any number to the exponent of 0 is equal to _____.

7. Jordi is trying to decide if the following table represents a geometric or arithmetic sequence.

x	$f(x)$
1	3
2	12
3	48
4	192

Part A: Is Jordi correct if she decides that this is an arithmetic sequence? Justify your answer.

Part B: Sketch the graph of the function.

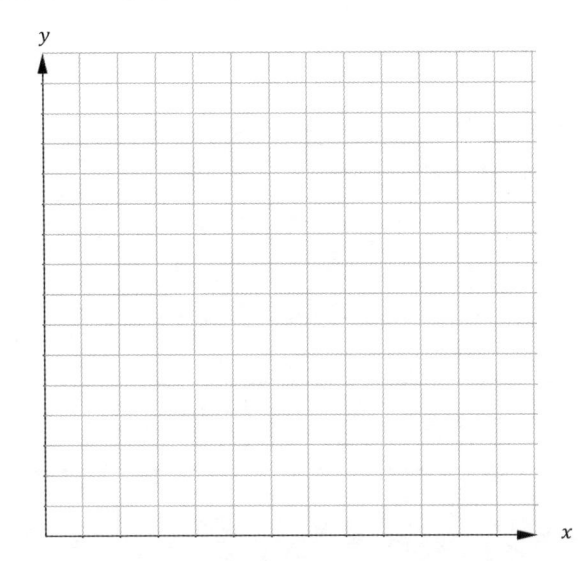

Section 7 – Topic 2
Exponential Functions

1. Given the following table and graph, write the equation to represent the exponential function.

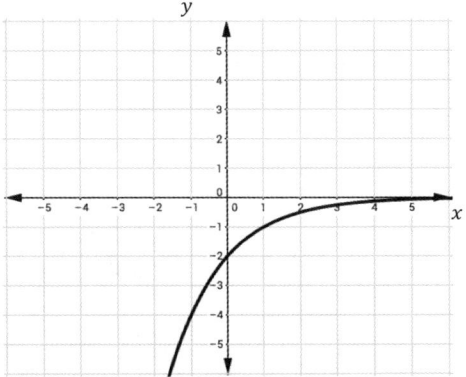

x	y
-1	-4
0	-2
1	-1
2	-0.5

2. Suppose you are performing an experiment in science class in which you start with 70 bacteria and the amount of bacteria triples every hour. Write a function to represent the growth of the bacteria over time in your science experiment.

3. Create a real-world scenario with a written description for the following numeric table:

x	$f(x)$
0	4
1	8
2	16
3	32

Practice Book - Section 7: Exponential Functions

4. In the equation for exponential functions, $y = a \cdot b^x$, how does the a term relate to a key feature of the graph?

5. Look at the following graph and explain how you know that the function being represented is not exponential.

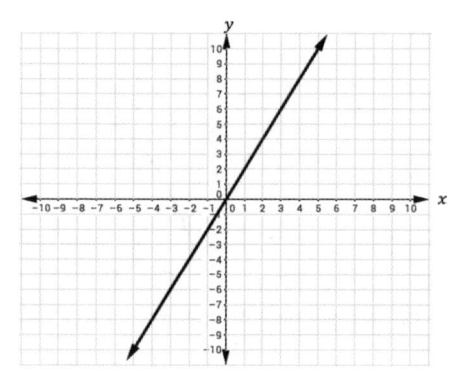

6. Write an equation for the exponential function represented in the table and graph below.

x	y
-2	1.5
-1	3
0	6
1	12
2	24

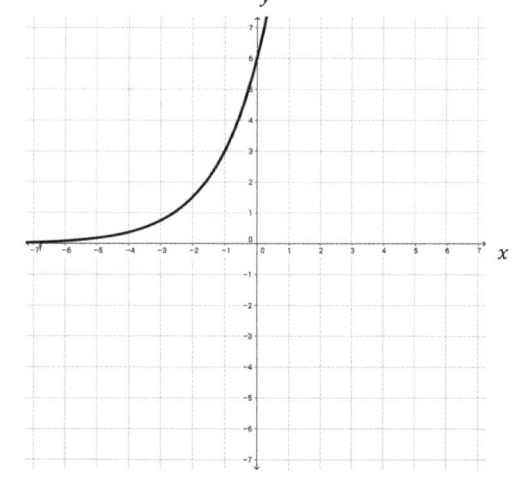

7. Match the graphs below with the following functions.

$f(x) = 2^x$

$f(x) = -2^x$

$f(x) = 3 \cdot 2^x$

$f(x) = -3 \cdot 2^x$

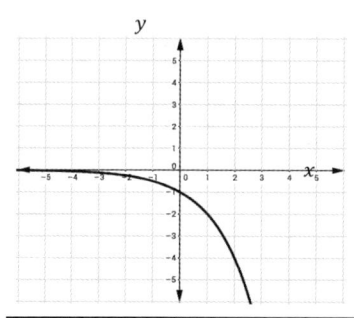

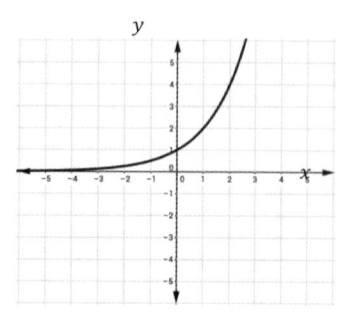

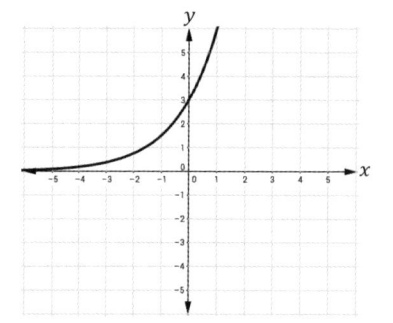

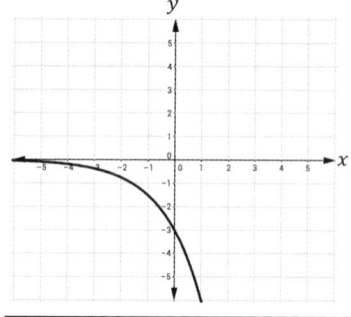

Practice Book - Section 7: Exponential Functions

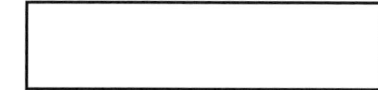

Section 7 – Topic 3
Graphs of Exponential Functions – Part 1

1. Sketch the graph of $f(x) = 3^x$ and describe the end behavior of the graph.

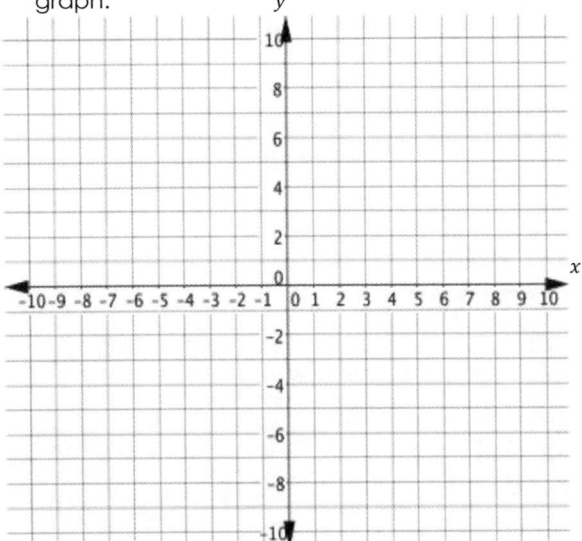

2. Sketch the graph of $f(x) = -3^x$ and describe the end behavior of the graph.

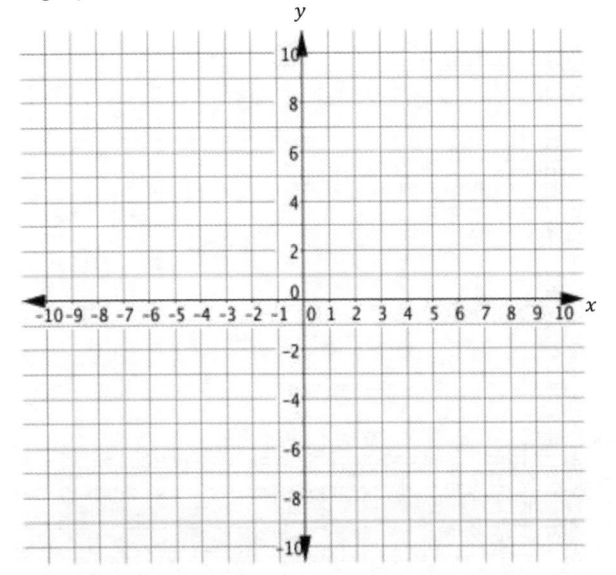

3. Sketch the graph of $f(x) = -\left(\frac{1}{3}\right)^x$ and describe the end behavior of the graph.

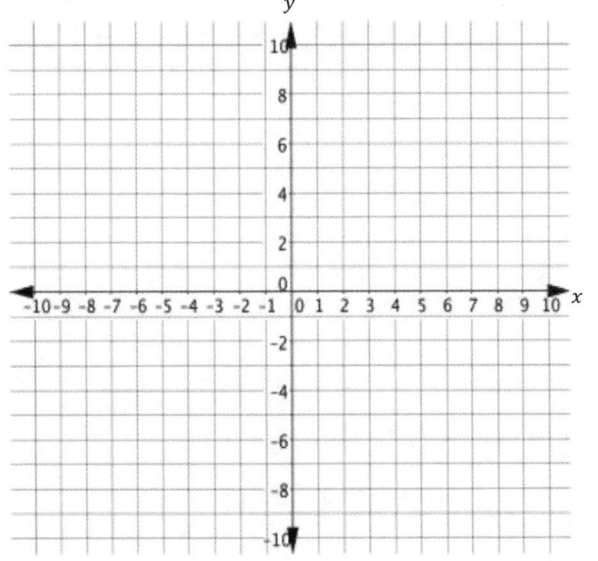

4. Consider the following function.

$$f(x) = 5^x$$

Complete the following statements about $f(x)$.

The y-intercept of $f(x)$ is _____.

The x-intercept of $f(x)$ is _____.

The end behavior of $f(x)$ is _____.

Practice Book - Section 7: Exponential Functions

5. Complete the following table for $h(x) = -\left(\frac{1}{4}\right)^x$

x	y
3	
−1	
0	
	−16
	−64

6. Consider the following function.

$$f(x) = 2 * 3^x$$

Complete the following statements about $f(x)$.

The y-intercept of $f(x)$ is _____.

The x-intercept of $f(x)$ is _____.

The end behavior of $f(x)$ is _____.

7. In the statement below, circle the correct word in each of the shaded segments.

If the y-intercept of an exponential function is positive and the common ratio (r) is between 0 and 1, then as x increases, y → 0 | y increases. If the y-intercept of an exponential function is negative and the common ratio (r) is greater than 1, then as x increases, y → 0 | y decreases.

Section 7 – Topic 4
Graphs of Exponential Functions – Part 2

1. Use the properties of exponents to sketch the graph of $f(x) = 2^{x+3}$. Describe the end behavior.

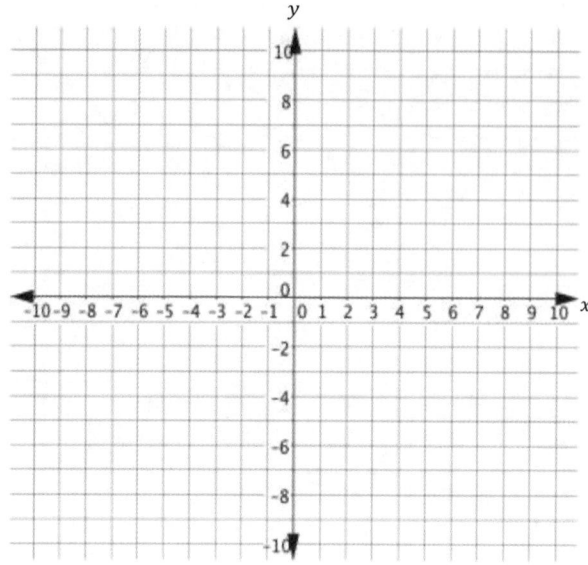

2. Use the properties of exponents to sketch the graph of $f(x) = -4 * 3^{x-1}$. Describe the end behavior.

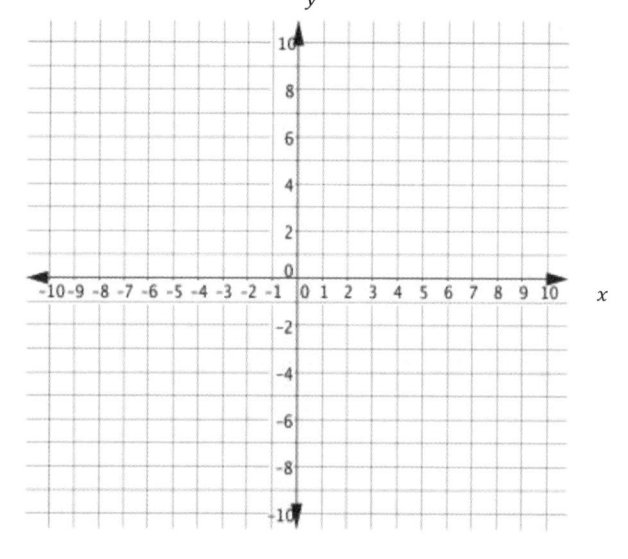

3. Which of the following would have the same graphic representation as the function $f(x) = 125 \cdot 5^x$? Select all that apply.

☐ $f(x) = 5 \cdot 5$
☐ $f(x) = 3^{6x}$
☐ $f(x) = 5^{x+3}$
☐ $f(x) = \frac{1}{25} 5^{x+5}$
☐ $f(x) = 25 \cdot 5^{x+1}$

4. Complete the following statements.

The graph that represents the function $f(x) = 2 \cdot 4^{x+1}$ has a y-intercept of _____. The graph is increasing by a common ratio of _____ and to the right is _____ and to the left is _____.

5. Which of the following would have the same graphic representation as the function $f(x) = 27 \cdot 3^x$? Select all that apply.

☐ $f(x) = 3 \cdot 3^{3x}$
☐ $f(x) = 3^{4x}$
☐ $f(x) = 3^{x+3}$
☐ $f(x) = (3^x)^3$
☐ $f(x) = 9 \cdot 3^{x+1}$

6. Consider the following function.

$$f(x) = -2(3)^{x-2}$$

Complete the following statements about $f(x)$.

The y-intercept of $f(x)$ is _____.

The x-intercept of $f(x)$ is _____.

The end behavior of $f(x)$ is _____.

$f(3) =$ _____

$f(4) =$ _____

Section 7 – Topic 5
Growth and Decay Rates of Exponential Functions

1. Consider the exponential function $f(x) = 250(1.03)^x$, which models Shawnda's savings account, where x represents the number of years since the money was invested.

   Part A: Is the money in the account growing or decaying?

   Part B: What is the rate of growth or decay?

   Part C: What does the value of 250 represent?

2. The exponential function $f(x) = 100\,(0.7)^x$ models

   ○ exponential growth
   ○ exponential decay

   and the rate of growth/decay is

   ○ 30%.
   ○ 70%.
   ○ 130%.

3. Write an exponential function to represent a situation in which the initial value is 175 and the rate of decay is 20%.

4. Consider the exponential function $f(x) = 13,500 \cdot 0.89^x$, which models the value of Mikayla's scooter, where x represents the number of years since she purchased the scooter.

Part A: Is the value of Mikayla's scooter growing or decaying?

Part B: What is the rate of growth or decay?

Part C: What does 13,500 represent?

Part D: What is the value of Mikayla's scooter after 4 years?

5. The function $f(x) = 200 \cdot 1.02^x$ models the amount of money in Jordan's savings account, where x represents the number of months since Jordan first placed his money into his account. Which of the following are true statements? Select all that apply.

- ☐ The function models exponential growth.
- ☐ 200 represents the amount of money Jordan put in his savings account in the beginning.
- ☐ The rate of decay is 2%.
- ☐ Jordan has $208.08 after the first month of his savings account.
- ☐ At the end of 4 months, Jordan will have more than $220 in savings.

Section 7 – Topic 6
Transformations of Exponential Functions

1. Consider the graph $f(x) = 3^x$. Describe how to graph the transformation $f(x - 3) + 2$.

2. The following is a graph of the function $f(x) = 2^x$. Graph the transformation $f(x + 3)$ on the blank coordinate axis.

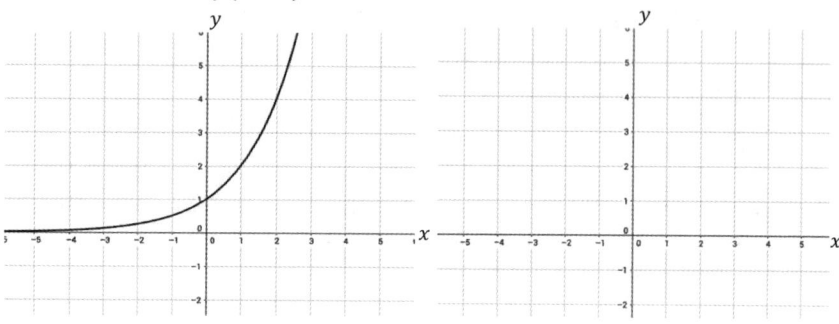

3. Sam claims that when he completes the transformation $f(x) + 3$, the parent function would move three units to the left.

Part A: Do you agree or disagree? Why or why not?

Part B: What misconception do you think Sam needs to clear up?

4. Describe how k affects the graph of the function $f(x) = 4^x$.

   Part A: $k \cdot f(x)$

   Part B: $f(x + k)$

   Part C: $f(x) + k$

6. Look at the following two graphs and write the exponential function for the transformation from the first graph to the second graph.

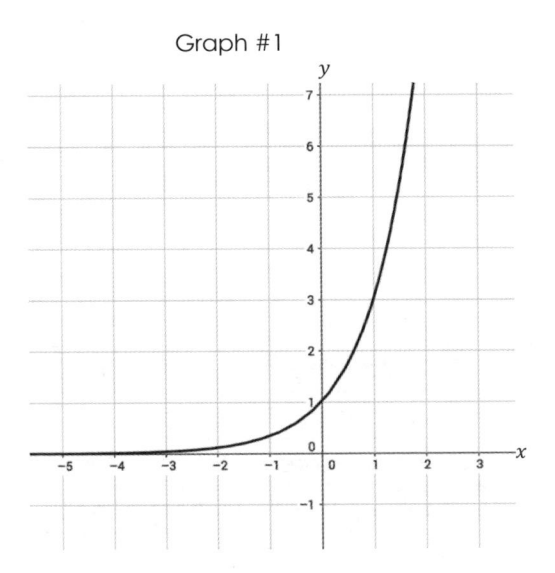

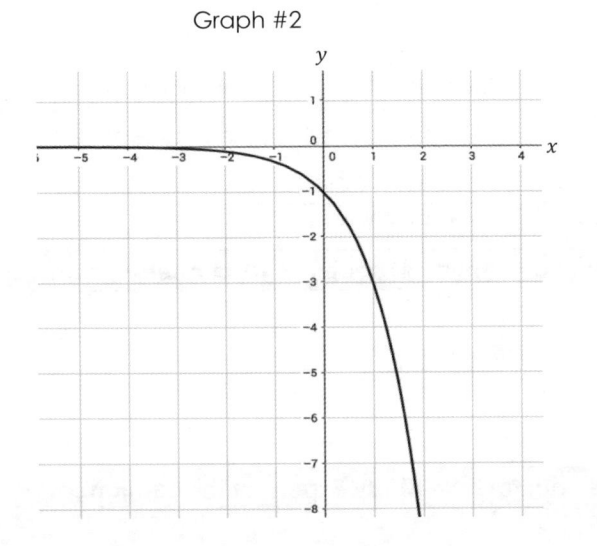

   Graph #1

   Graph #2

5. Consider the following function notation transformations using. $f(x) = 4^x$ as the parent function. Describe what happens in each transformation.

$f(x - 2)$	
$f(x) + 2$	
$3f(x)$	
4^{x+4}	
$4^x - 3$	

Practice Book - Section 7: Exponential Functions

Section 8: Summary of Functions
Student Learning Plan

Topic Number	Topic Name	Date Completed	Study Expert(s)	Check Your Understanding Score
1	Comparing Linear, Quadratic, and Exponential Functions – Part 1			
2	Comparing Linear, Quadratic, and Exponential Functions – Part 2			
3	Comparing Arithmetic and Geometric Sequences			
4	Exploring Non-Arithmetic, Non-Geometric Sequences			
5	Modeling with Functions			
6	Understanding Piecewise-Defined Functions			
7	Absolute Value Functions			
8	Graphing Power Functions – Part 1			
9	Graphing Power Functions – Part 2			
10	Finding Zeros of Polynomial Functions of Higher Degree			
11	End Behavior of Graphs of Polynomial Functions			
12	Graphing Polynomial Functions of Higher Degree			
13	Recognizing Even and Odd Functions			
14	Solutions to Systems of Functions			
Honors 1	Arithmetic and Geometric Sequences			
Honors 2	Inverse Functions			

*Honors resources are available online.

What did you learn in this section? What questions do you still have?

Who was your favorite Study Expert for this section? Why?

Section 8 – Topic 1
Comparing Linear, Quadratic, and Exponential Functions – Part 1

1. Consider the following graphs and choose the correct name of each function.

    Part A:

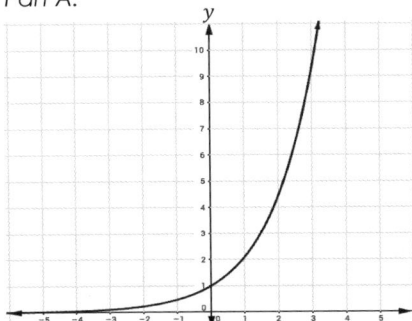

    Ⓐ Linear function
    Ⓑ Absolute value function
    Ⓒ Quadratic function
    Ⓓ Exponential function
    Ⓔ Square root function

    Part B:

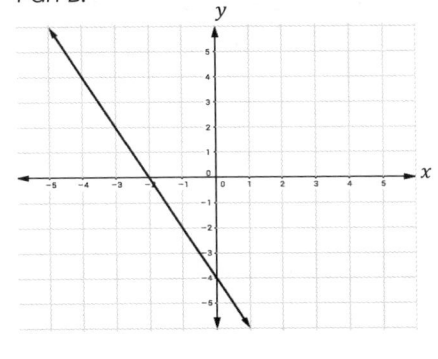

    Ⓐ Linear function
    Ⓑ Absolute value function
    Ⓒ Quadratic function
    Ⓓ Exponential function
    Ⓔ Square root function

    Part C:

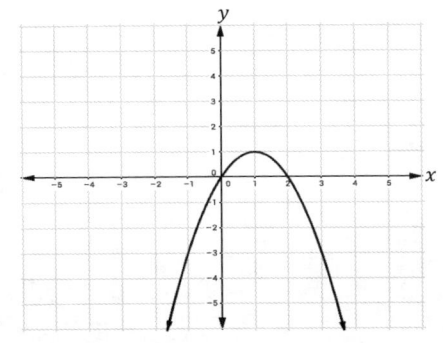

    Ⓐ Linear function
    Ⓑ Absolute value function
    Ⓒ Quadratic function
    Ⓓ Exponential function
    Ⓔ Square root function

2. Consider the following graph.

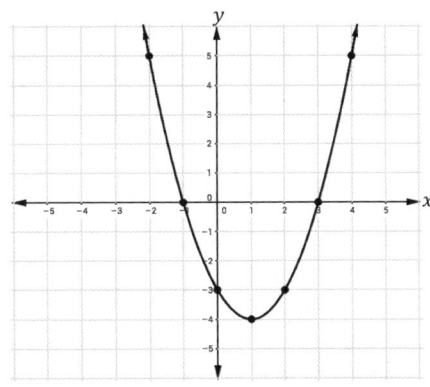

    Part A: Circle the word that correctly completes the following statement.

    The function represented in the above graph is exponential | quadratic.

    Part B: The a value of the function represented in the graph above is

    ○ positive
    ○ negative
    ○ zero

    because

    Part C: The c value of the function represented in the graph above is

    ○ positive
    ○ negative
    ○ zero

    because

    Part D: Write the equation that would represent the graph shown above.

Practice Book - Section 8: Summary of Functions

3. Determine whether the rate of change for each function is constant or not constant.

   Part A: The rate of change for a linear function is
   - ○ constant.
   - ○ not constant.

   Part B: The rate of change for an exponential function is
   - ○ constant.
   - ○ not constant.

   Part C: The rate of change for a quadratic function is
   - ○ constant.
   - ○ not constant.

4. Consider the table below that represents a quadratic function.

x	$f(x)$
−3	4.5
−2	2
0	0
2	2
3	4.5

   Part A: What is the rate of change between the first and second point?

   Part B: What is the rate of change between the second and third point?

   Part C: What is the rate of change between the third and fourth point?

   Part D: What is the rate of change between the fourth and fifth point?

5. Use the pattern of the rate of change to complete the table below that represents a linear function.

x	y
−2	8
−1	5
0	2
1	−1
2	
3	

Practice Book - Section 8: Summary of Functions

Section 8 – Topic 2
Comparing Linear, Quadratic, and Exponential Functions – Part 2

1. Determine whether each table represents a linear, quadratic, or exponential function and justify your answer. Write the correct function name and justification next to the corresponding table.

Part A:

x	y
0	5
1	0
2	−3
3	−4
4	−3

Part B:

x	y
2	5
5	14
6	17
8	23
10	29

Part C:

x	y
−3	8
−2	4
−1	2
0	1
1	$\frac{1}{2}$

2. Identify whether the following real-world examples should be modeled by a linear, quadratic, or exponential function.

Real-World Example	Linear	Quadratic	Exponential
Each ink cartridge purchased for a printer costs $12	○	○	○
Throwing a ball	○	○	○
The amount of money you earn when you get paid an hourly wage	○	○	○
A bank account balance earning an annual interest rate	○	○	○
Maximizing the area of a rectangular fenced area in a large field	○	○	○
Population growth of a city	○	○	○

3. Complete the following table so that $f(x)$ represents a linear function and $g(x)$ represents an exponential function.

x	$f(x)$	$g(x)$
−2	6	$\frac{1}{9}$
−1		$\frac{1}{3}$
0	14	
1		
2		

4. Determine the function(s) whose domain are all real numbers. Choose all that apply.

    ☐ Linear function
    ☐ Quadratic function
    ☐ Exponential function

5. Determine the function(s) whose graph has a vertex. Choose all that apply.

    ☐ Linear function
    ☐ Quadratic function
    ☐ Exponential function

6. What is the maximum number of times that a quadratic function can intersect the x-axis?

7. What type of symmetry can the graph of a quadratic function have?

    Ⓐ Symmetry about the x-axis
    Ⓑ Symmetry about the y-axis
    Ⓒ Symmetry about the line $y = x$
    Ⓓ No symmetry

Section 8 – Topic 3
Comparing Arithmetic and Geometric Sequences

1. The Gaineys and the Arnolds are saving money for a trip to Utah to go snowboarding. The Arnolds are going to save a nickel on the first day of the month and then double the amount each day for a month. The Gaineys are going to start their savings by saving $10 on the first day and then $10 each day of the month.

Part A: Write a recursive and explicit formula for each option.

The Arnold Family:

The Gainey Family:

Part B: Complete the following tables for the two options.

The Arnolds:

Day	Savings
1	
2	
3	
4	
5	
30	

The Gaineys:

Day	Savings
1	
2	
3	
4	
5	
30	

Part C: Given the two options, which is a better savings option?

Part D: Which option should you choose if you were only saving for 6 days?

Part E: Are these functions discrete or continuous? Justify your answer.

2. Korey starts a small carwash business to save up some cash. He decides to offer two different price packages to his clients. Package A charges $15.00 for the first car wash and a dollar less for each car wash after. Package B charges $28.00 for the first car wash, but the price is cut by 25% for each of the next car washes.

   Part A: Which car wash do you think you would choose as a customer and why would you pick that package?

Part B: List the prices for the first 8 carwashes of each package below.

Package A	
1	
2	
3	
4	
5	
6	
7	
8	

Package B	
1	
2	
3	
4	
5	
6	
7	
8	

Part C: Graph both Package A and Package B. Identify each graph as arithmetic or geometric.

Package A

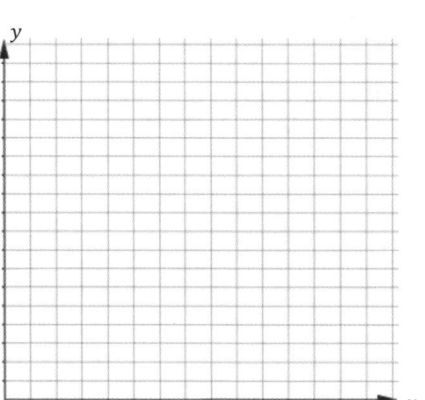

Package B

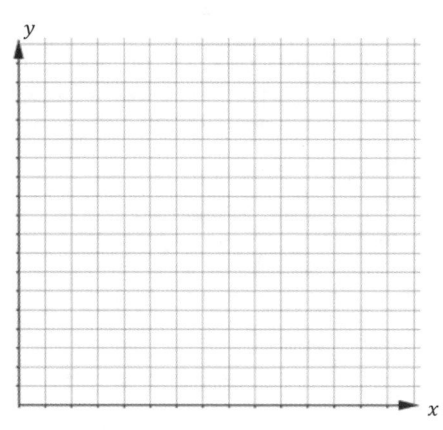

Practice Book - Section 8: Summary of Functions

Part D: If you think you will need 3 car washes, which package should you choose? Why?

Part E: If you think you will need 7 car washes, which package should you choose? Why?

Part F: Korey will allow customers to use each package until the price of a car wash reaches $2.00. How many car washes does Package A allow? How many car washes does Package B allow?

Section 8 – Topic 4
Exploring Non-Arithmetic, Non-Geometric Sequences

1. Determine whether the following sequences are arithmetic, geometric, or neither.

Sequence	Arithmetic	Geometric	Neither
8, 16, 24, 32, 40 ...	○	○	○
1, 1, 3, 4, 5, 8 ...	○	○	○
1, 4, 16, 64, 256 ...	○	○	○
−3, 3, 13, 27, 45	○	○	○
5, 6, 7, 8, 9, 10 ...	○	○	○
4, 2, 1, $\frac{1}{2}, \frac{1}{4}, \frac{1}{16}$	○	○	○

2. Consider a sequence where $f(1) = 1, f(2) = 3$, and $f(n) = f(n-1) + f(n-2)$.

   Part A: List the first 5 terms of this sequence.

   Part B: Why is it necessary to state the first two terms before stating the rest of the formula in order to determine the rest of the terms in the sequence?

3. Consider the following sequence.

$$6, 13, 23, 36, 52 \ldots$$

Part A: Complete the table below for the sequence.

n	$f(x)$

Part B: Find the first and second differences for this sequence using the table above. What kind of function does this sequence appear to represent?

Part C: What are the domain restrictions on this function?

Part D: Write the recursive formula for this function in the form $f(x) = f(x-1) + mx + b$, using the second difference as the linear rate of change (m), and using values from the table to determine b.

4. Complete the following table that represents a sequence with a second difference of four.

n	$f(x)$
1	8
2	12
3	
4	
5	

Practice Book - Section 8: Summary of Functions

Section 8 – Topic 5
Modeling with Functions

1. Consider the following diagram that displays the modeling cycle process.

   Part A: Complete the diagram.

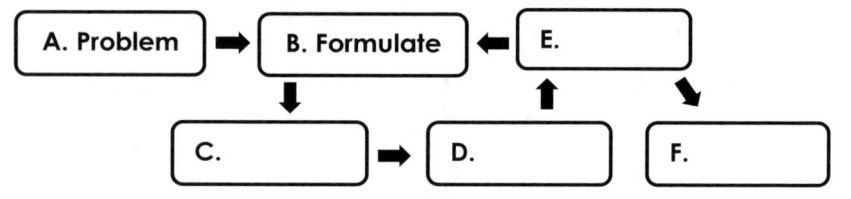

   ```
   A. Problem  →  B. Formulate  ←  E.
                     ↓         ↑      ↘
                    C.    →    D.       F.
   ```

   Part B: In the examples below, determine the step in the cycle that each statement demonstrates, and write the letter of the corresponding part of the cycle (from the diagram above).

   I. The results tell us that the number of bees in the park has been decreasing at a constant rate for the last eight years. _____

   II. The function that models the table is $f(x) = x^2 + 40$, where x is the number of years since an afterschool program was developed, and y is the number of students enrolled. This means that in 15 years, there will be 265 students enrolled in the afterschool program. _____

   III. The relationship between variables can best be represented with an exponential model. _____

   IV. In conclusion, the scores increased for students that completed test corrections and stayed constant or decreased for students that did not complete test corrections. _____

   V. The variables are the number of employees and the amount of money earned. _____

   VI. The function accurately matches the graph. _____

2. James folds a piece of paper in half several times, each time unfolding the paper to count how many equal parts he sees. After folding the paper about six times, it becomes too difficult to fold it again, but he is curious how many parts the paper would be broken into if he could continue to fold it. He decides to employ the modeling cycle to predict how many parts the paper would be folded into if he were able to fold it 11 times.

x	0	1	2	3	4	5	6
$f(x)$	1	2	4	8	16	32	64

   Part A: What are the variables in this situation and what do they represent?

   Part B: What type of function models this context? How do you know?

   Part C: Sketch a graph and find the function that models the table.

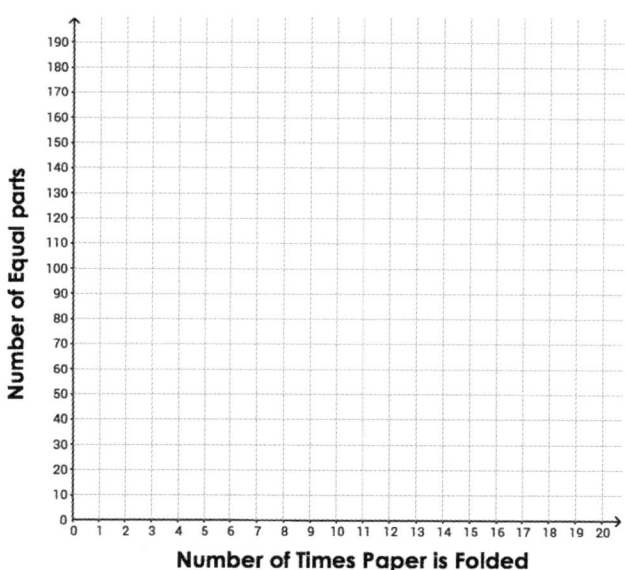

   (Graph with y-axis labeled "Number of Equal parts" from 0 to 190, and x-axis labeled "Number of Times Paper is Folded" from 0 to 20.)

126 Practice Book - Section 8: Summary of Functions

Part D: Use the function to predict the number of equal parts that the paper would be folded into if it were possible to fold it 11 times.

Part E: Based on the results, why do you think James could no longer fold the paper after about 6 folds?

Part F: What methods can we use to validate the conclusions for this function model?

Part G: What key elements should be included in James's report?

Section 8 – Topic 6
Understanding Piecewise-Defined Functions

1. Consider the following piecewise function and the graph that represents the function.

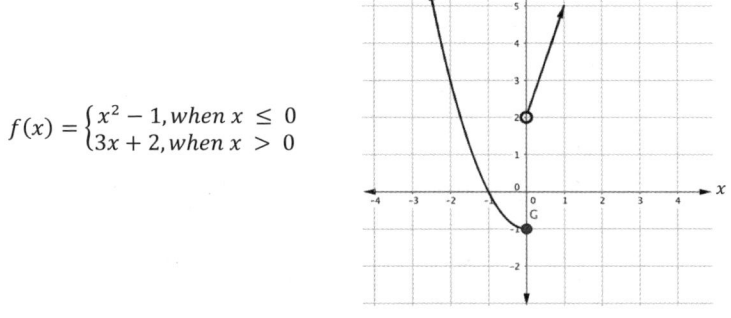

$$f(x) = \begin{cases} x^2 - 1, \text{when } x \leq 0 \\ 3x + 2, \text{when } x > 0 \end{cases}$$

Part A: Label the pieces of the $f(x)$ on the graph.

Part B: What does the closed circle represent?

Part C: What does the open circle represent?

Part D: Give the domain for which the graph is linear.

Part E: Give the domain for which the graph is nonlinear (curved).

2. Students at a local high school in New York City were reviewing piecewise functions as part of the NY State Common Core Mathematics Curriculum tutoring program. They came across this graph.

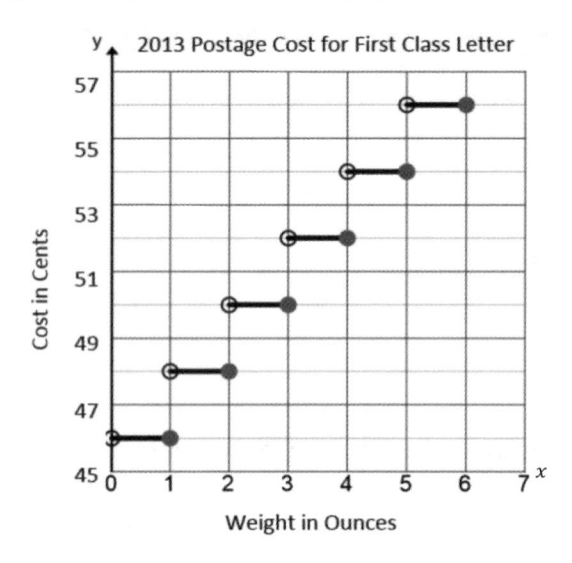

Part A: How many pieces are in the step function?

Part B: How many intervals make up the step function? What are the interval values?

Part C: Why do we use open circles in some situations and closed circles in others?

Part D: How do you know this is a function?

Part E: Are the pieces of this piecewise function linear or nonlinear?

Part F: What is the range of this piecewise function?

3. *Fluffy Dreams*, an inflatables indoor park, is open 7 days a week for 14 hours a day. Their prices are listed below:

2 hours or less: $12
Between 2 and 6 hours: $19
6 or more hours: $25

The following piecewise function represents their prices:

$$f(x) = \begin{cases} 12, \text{when } 0 < x \leq 2 \\ 19, \text{when } 2 < x < 6 \\ 25, \text{when } 6 \leq x \leq 14 \end{cases}$$

Graph the function on the coordinate plane below.

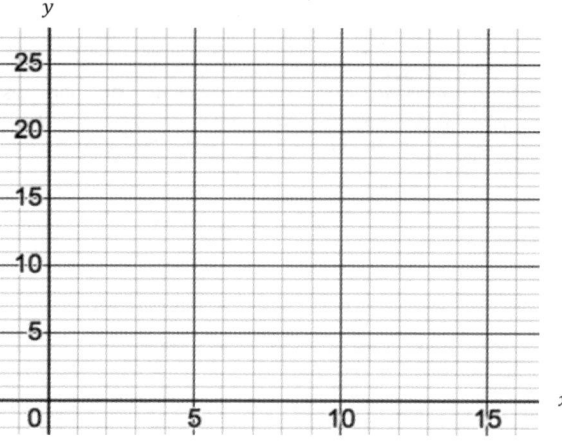

4. Choose the correct expression to represent the piecewise function.

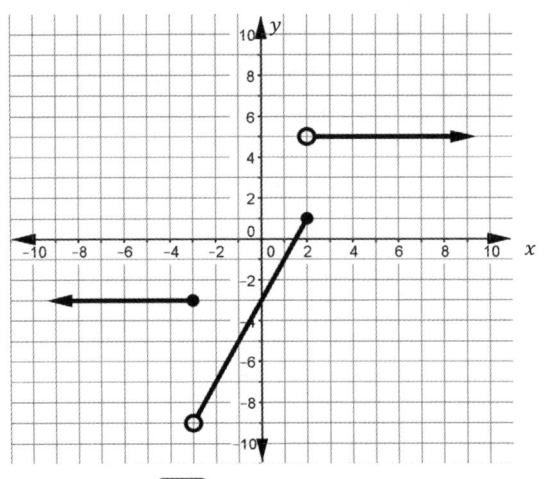

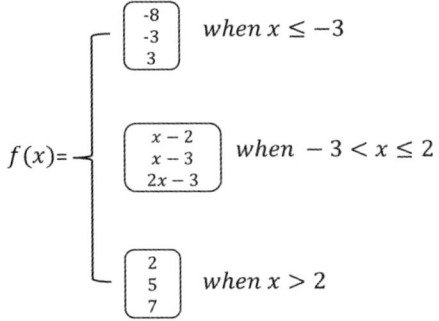

$$f(x) = \begin{cases} \boxed{\begin{array}{c}-8\\-3\\3\end{array}} & \text{when } x \leq -3 \\ \boxed{\begin{array}{c}x-2\\x-3\\2x-3\end{array}} & \text{when } -3 < x \leq 2 \\ \boxed{\begin{array}{c}2\\5\\7\end{array}} & \text{when } x > 2 \end{cases}$$

5. Evaluate the piecewise-defined function for the given values of x by matching the domain values with the range values.

$$f(x) = \begin{cases} -2x+1, & x \leq -3 \\ 3x-1, & -3 < x \leq 5 \\ x+5, & x > 5 \end{cases}$$

−7	2
−3	7
1	13
5	14
8	15

Section 8 – Topic 7
Absolute Value Functions

1. Consider the absolute value function: $f(x) = |x| - 2$.

   Part A: Sketch the graph of $f(x)$ by completing the table of values.

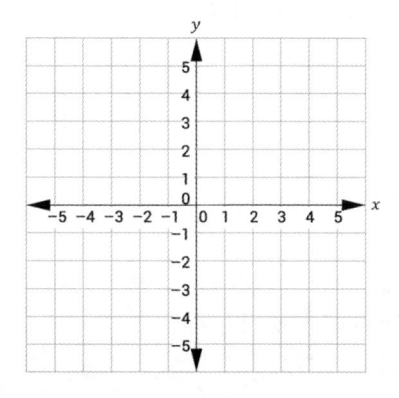

x	$f(x)$
−2	
−1	
0	
1	
2	

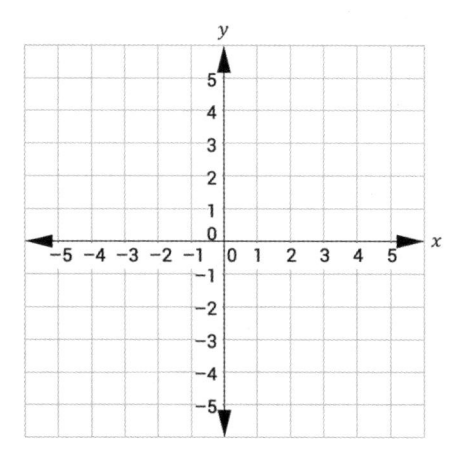

   Part B: Write $f(x)$ as a piecewise-defined function.

2. Sketch the graph $h(x) = |x - 1| - 1$.

   Part A: Sketch the graph of $h(x)$ by completing the table of values.

x	$h(x)$
−2	
−1	
0	
1	
2	

Practice Book - Section 8: Summary of Functions

129

Part B: Write $h(x)$ as a piecewise-defined function.

3. Consider the function below.

$$t(x) = \begin{cases} -x - 4, \text{ when } x < -3 \\ x + 2, \text{ when } x \geq -3 \end{cases}$$

Write the absolute value function that represents $t(x)$.

4. Compare and contrast $f(x)$ and $g(x)$.

$$f(x) = |x + 2| + 1 \qquad g(x) = \begin{cases} -x - 3, \text{ when } x < -2 \\ x + 1, \text{ when } x \geq -2 \end{cases}$$

5. Consider the following piecewise-defined function.

$$s(x) = \begin{cases} -x - 4, \text{ when } x < -2 \\ x, \text{ when } x \geq -2 \end{cases}$$

Which of the following functions also represents $s(x)$?

Ⓐ $f(x) = |x + 2| + 2$
Ⓑ $h(x) = |-x - 4| + 2$
Ⓒ $m(x) = |x + 2| - 2$
Ⓓ $n(x) = |x| - 4$

6. Consider the figures $f(x)$, $h(x)$, $q(x)$, and $w(x)$ in the graph below.

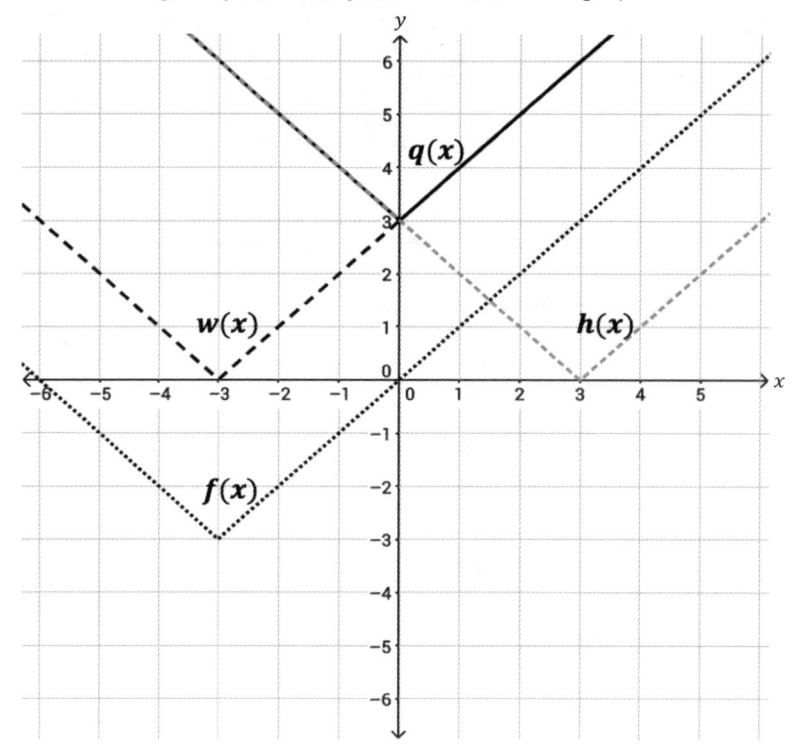

Match each of the following functions with the name of the corresponding figure from the graph.

_____	$|-x + 3|$	**A.** $f(x)$
_____	$|x| + 3$	**B.** $h(x)$
_____	$|x + 3|$	**C.** $q(x)$
_____	$|x + 3| - 3$	**D.** $w(x)$

Section 8 – Topic 8
Graphing Power Functions – Part 1

1. Consider the following function $m(x) = \sqrt{x} + 3$.

   Part A: Sketch the graph of $m(x)$ on the axes below.

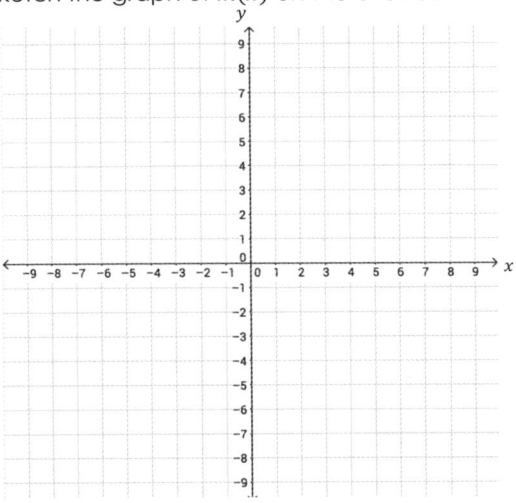

   Part B: Describe the domain and range of $m(x)$.

2. Consider the function $h(x) = \sqrt[3]{x} - 1$.

   Part A: Sketch the graph of $h(x)$ on the axes below.

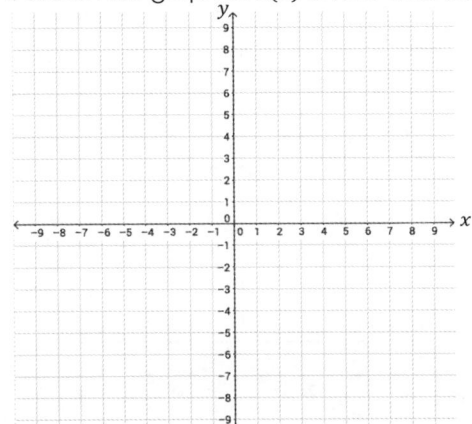

   Part B: Describe the domain and range of $h(x)$.

3. Consider the following functions.

   $$F(x) = \sqrt[3]{x} + 2$$

   $$G(x) = \sqrt{x} - 2$$

   Part A: Sketch the graphs of $F(x)$ and $G(x)$ on the axes below.

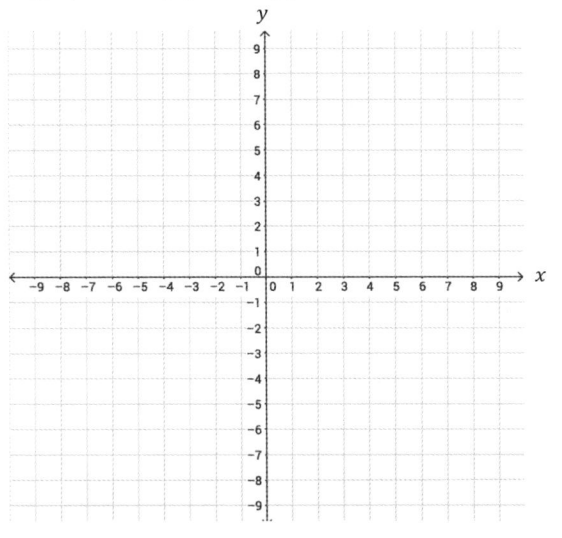

   Part B: In the statement below, circle the correct word(s) in each of the shaded segments to accurately describe the functions.

   $F(x)$ is an example of a square root | cube root function.

   $G(x)$ is an example of a square root | cube root function.

   $F(x)$ and $G(x)$ are both examples of exponential | quadratic | power functions.

   Part C: Compare and contrast the domain and range of $F(x)$ and $G(x)$.

Practice Book - Section 8: Summary of Functions

Section 8 – Topic 9
Graphing Power Functions – Part 2

1. Consider the following function.

$$f(x) = x^3 - 2$$

Part A: Sketch the graph of $f(x)$ on the set of axes below.

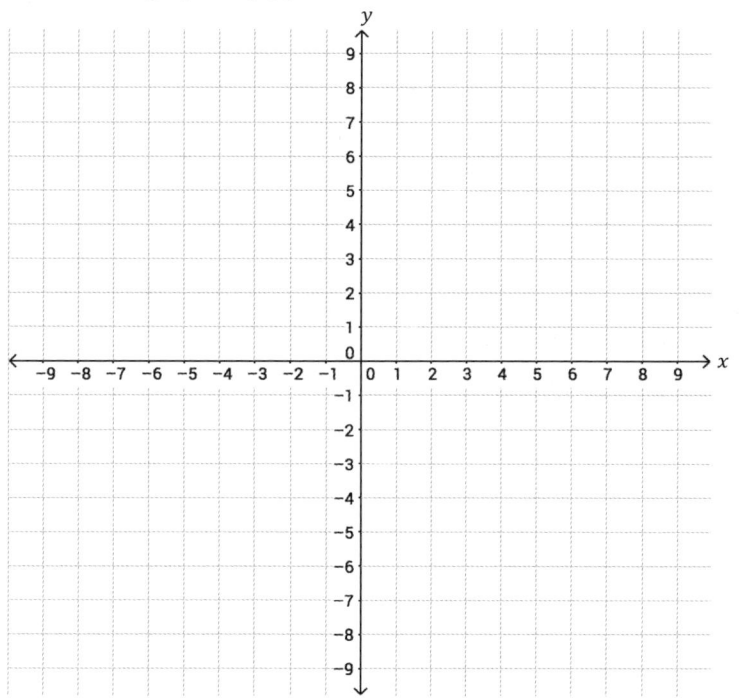

Part B: Describe the domain and range of $f(x)$.

2. Consider the functions $f(x) = \sqrt{x}$, $g(x) = \sqrt[3]{x}$, and $h(x) = x^3$. Complete the chart below by stating the correct name and characteristics for each graph.

Function Name ($f(x), g(x),$ or $h(x)$)	Graph of Function	Kind of Function (Cube Root, Square Root, or Cubic)	Domain and Range of function

3. Consider the functions below.
$$m(x) = x^3 - 5$$
$$r(x) = \sqrt[3]{x} - 5$$

Part A: Sketch the graph of both functions on the coordinate plane below.

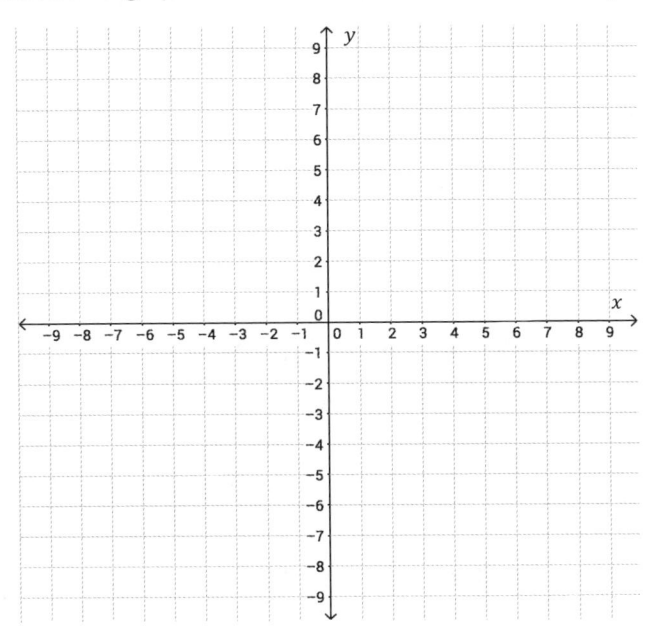

Part B: Compare and contrast $m(x)$ and $r(x)$.

4. Hannah is giving her sister a softball for her birthday and wants to put it in a cubic gift box to preserve the surprise. She will fill the empty space in the box with packing peanuts so that the softball doesn't roll around. If the volume of the softball is 29 cubic inches, which equation models the relationship between the length of each side of the box (s) and the amount of empty space inside?

Ⓐ $E(s) = s^3$
Ⓑ $E(s) = s^3 - 29$
Ⓒ $E(s) = \sqrt[3]{s} - 29$
Ⓓ $E(s) = \sqrt{s}$

Section 8 – Topic 10
Finding Zeros of Polynomial Functions of Higher Degree

1. Consider the following graph of $f(x)$.

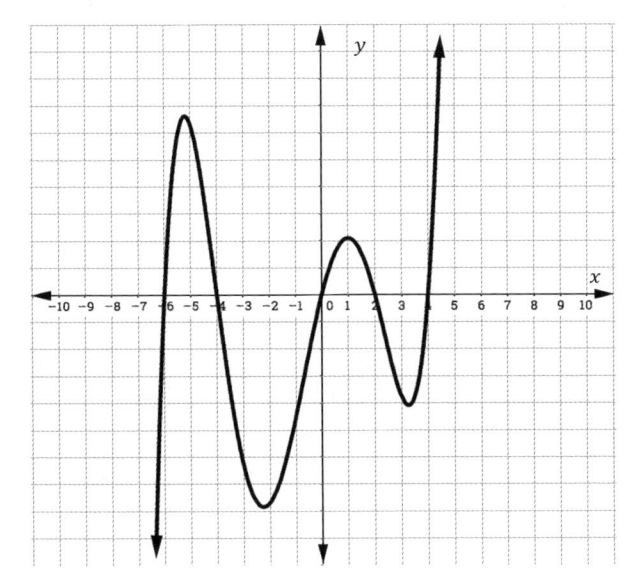

   What are the zeros of $f(x)$?

2. What are the zeros of $g(x) = (3x - 1)(2x + 5)(7x - 14)^2$?

Practice Book - Section 8: Summary of Functions

3. Which of the graphs has the same zeros as the function $f(x) = 2x^3 + 3x^2 - 9x$?

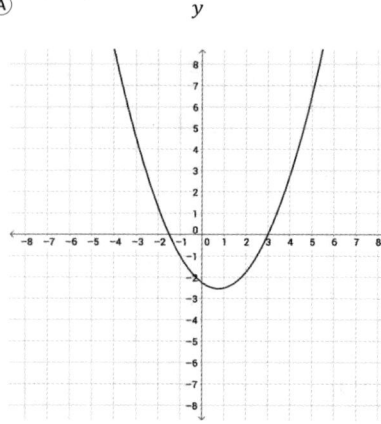

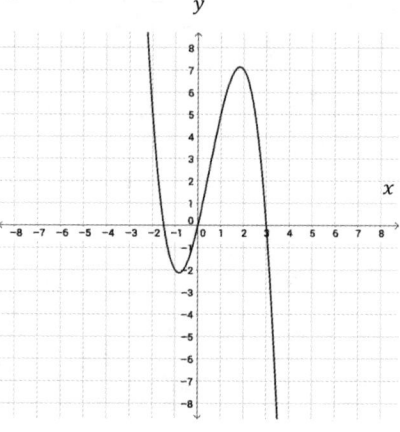

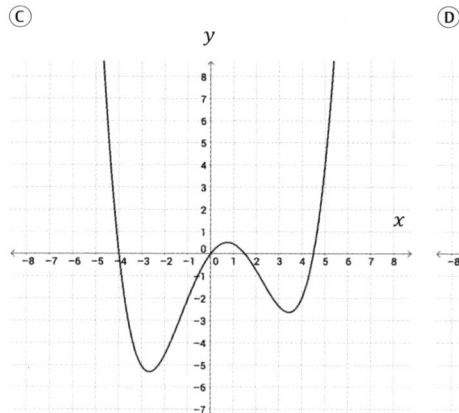

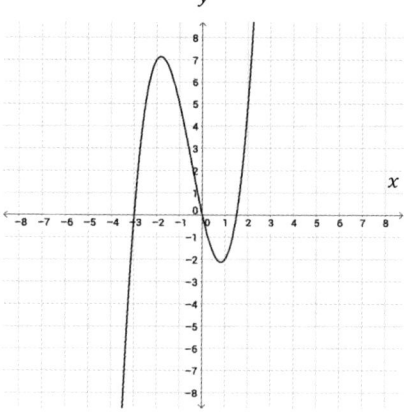

Ⓐ

Ⓑ

Ⓒ

Ⓓ

4. What are the zeros of $g(x) = x(x^2 - 25)(x^2 - 3x - 4)$?

5. Consider the function $k(x) = x^3 - 5x^2 - 24x$.

   Part A: Find the range of $k(x)$ for the given domain $\{6, 7, 8, 9\}$.

   Part B: Which value from *Part A* represents a zero of $k(x)$? Justify your answer.

   Part C: Determine the other zeros of $k(x)$ by factoring.

6. The graph of $t(x)$ is shown below.

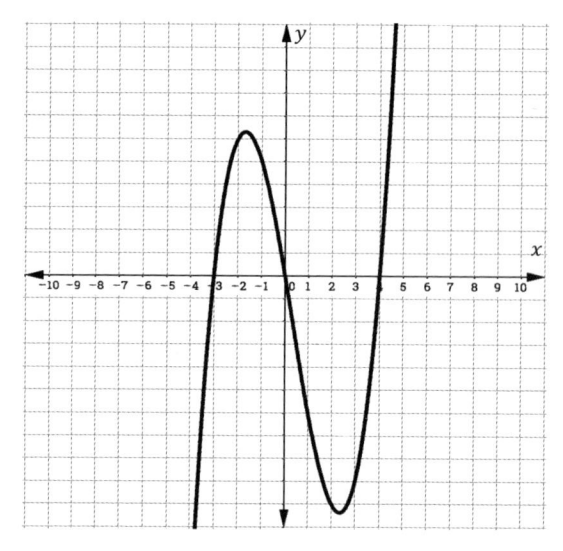

Section 8 – Topic 11
End Behavior of Graphs of Polynomial Functions

1. Describe the end behavior of the following graphs.

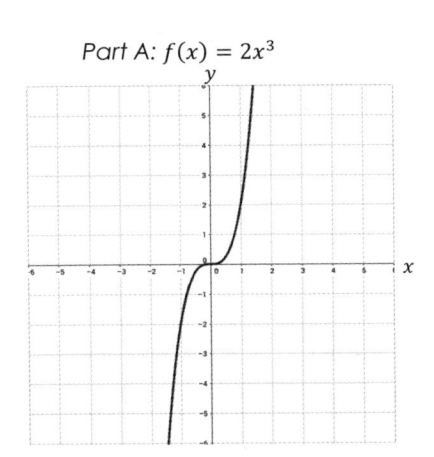

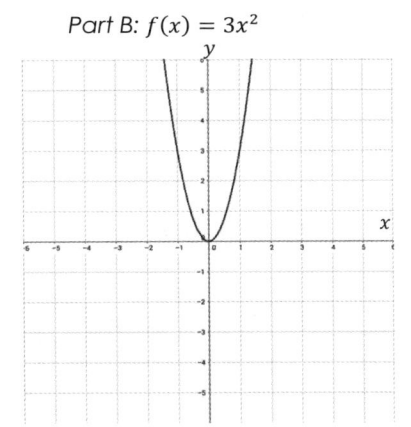

   Part A: $f(x) = 2x^3$

   Part B: $f(x) = 3x^2$

   Part C: $f(x) = -x^4$

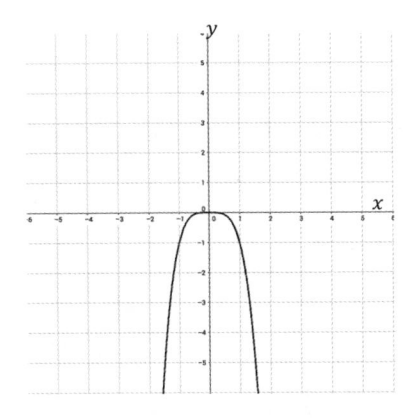

   Part D: $f(x) = x^5 - 1$

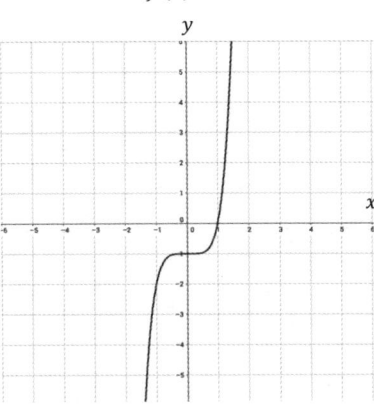

2. Complete the following sentence.

   If the leading coefficient is _____ and the exponent is _____, then the end behavior is described by as $x \to \infty, y \to -\infty$ and $x \to -\infty, y \to -\infty$.

3. Consider the following graph of $f(x)$.

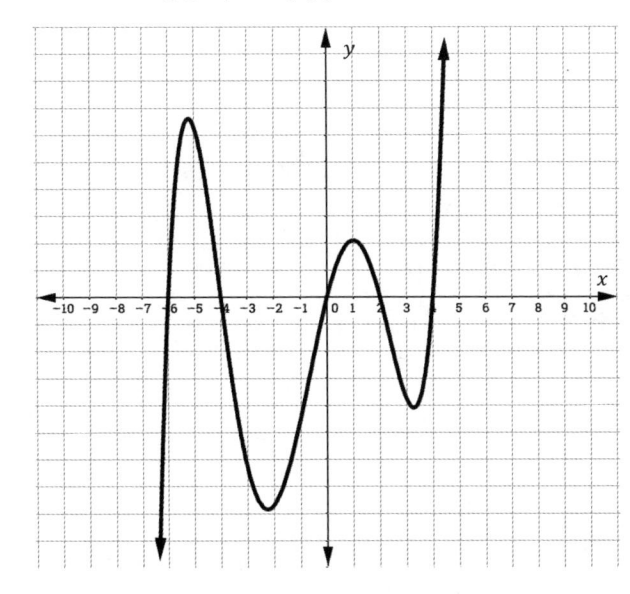

   Part A: Does the leading coefficient of the function $f(x)$ have an even or odd degree? Justify your answer.

   Part B: Is the leading coefficient of $f(x)$ positive or negative? Justify your answer.

Practice Book - Section 8: Summary of Functions

135

4. Describe the end behavior of the function $j(x) = -7x^4 - 3x^2 + 6x - 5 + x^5$.

   As $x \to \infty, f(x)$ _____

   As $x \to -\infty, f(x)$ _____

5. Determine which of the following statements is true for the function $f(x) = -6x^7 + 3x^8 - 1064$?

   Ⓐ As $x \to \infty, f(x) \to \infty$ and as $x \to -\infty, f(x) \to \infty$
   Ⓑ As $x \to \infty, f(x) \to -\infty$ and as $x \to -\infty, f(x) \to -\infty$
   Ⓒ As $x \to \infty, f(x) \to -\infty$ and as $x \to -\infty, f(x) \to \infty$
   Ⓓ As $x \to \infty, f(x) \to \infty$ and as $x \to -\infty, f(x) \to -\infty$

Section 8 – Topic 12
Graphing Polynomial Functions of Higher Degree

1. Consider the function $f(x) = x(x - 2)(x + 3)$.

   Part A: Describe the end behavior of the graph of $f(x)$.

   Part B: Find the zeros of $f(x)$.

   Part C: Use the end behavior and zeros to sketch the graph of $f(x)$ below.

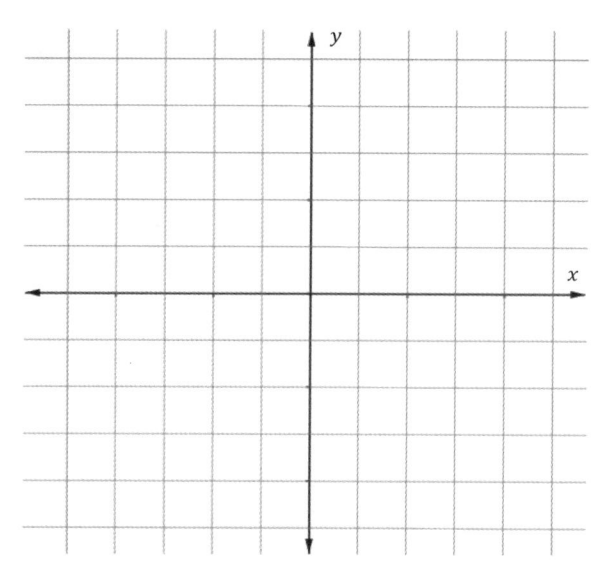

2. Sketch the graph of $f(x) = -(x-4)(x-1)(x+5)$.

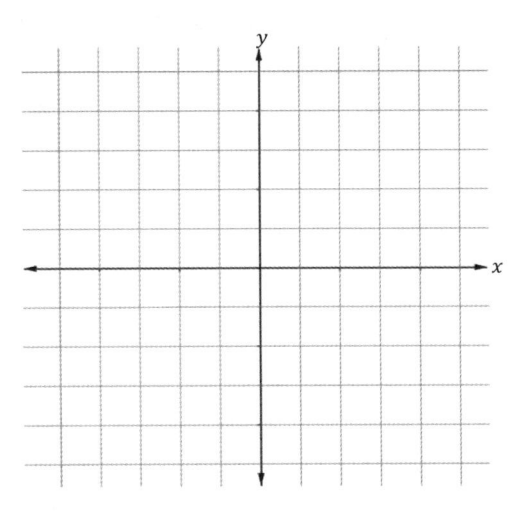

3. Sketch the graph of $f(x) = -x(2x-1)(x+4)$.

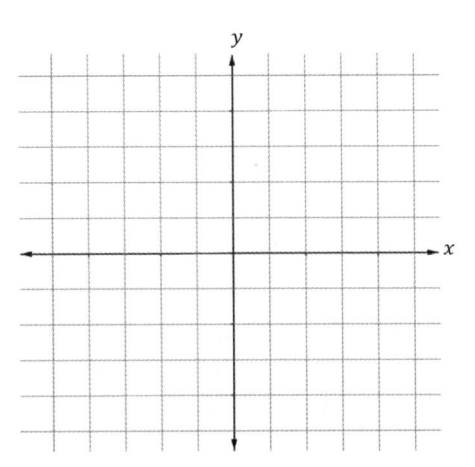

4. Match each equation with its corresponding graph.

A. $y = -(x-8)(x+7)(x-2)$ **B.** $y = (x+1)(x-7)(x+8)$

C. $y = -(x-2)(x+7)(x-8)(x+1)$ **D.** $y = (x-7)(x+8)(x-2)(x+1)$

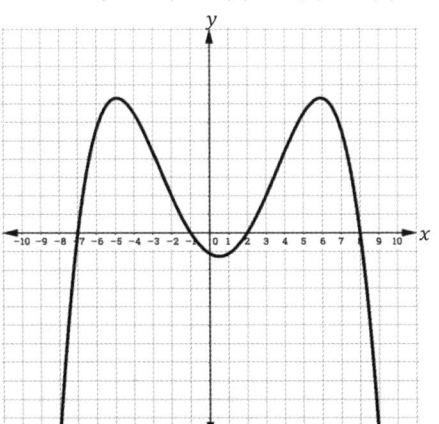

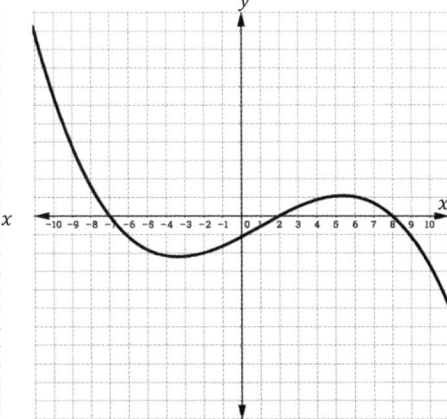

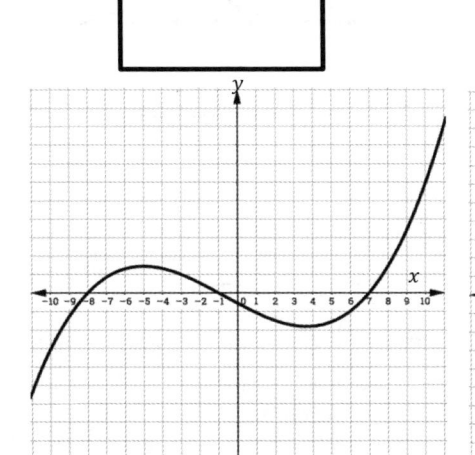

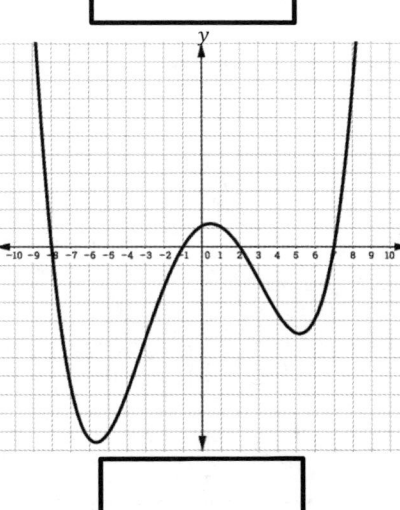

Practice Book - Section 8: Summary of Functions

137

Section 8 – Topic 13
Recognizing Even and Odd Functions

1. Consider the following graphs. Label each graph as even, odd, or neither in the space provided.

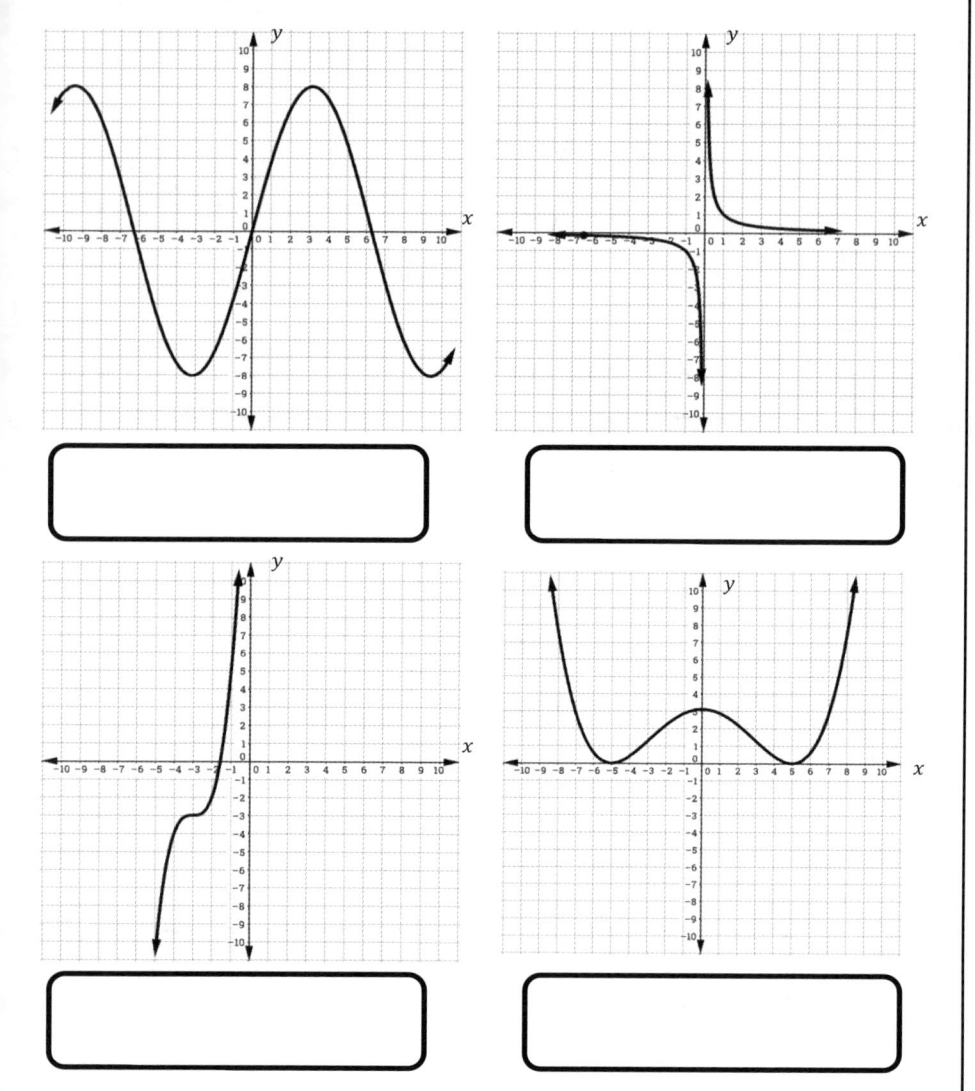

2. Determine if the following functions are even, odd, or neither.

Function	Even	Odd	Neither
$f(x) = x^2 + 1$	☐	☐	☐
$g(x) = (x^4 + 7)$	☐	☐	☐
$h(x) = 0$	☐	☐	☐
$j(x) = x + 6$	☐	☐	☐

3. Determine the values of $k, m,$ and n that create an odd function when plugged into $p(x) = x^k - x^m + n$. Justify your answer.

  Ⓐ $k = 4, m = 2,$ and $n = 1$

  Ⓑ $k = 3, m = 1,$ and $n = 9$

  Ⓒ $k = 7, m = 5,$ and $n = 2$

  Ⓓ None of the combinations above will create an odd function for $p(x)$.

4. Complete the statements.

  ➢ If a function is even, then $f(-x) = $ _____ and has symmetry about the _____.

  ➢ If a function is odd, then $f(-x) = $ _____ and has symmetry about the _____.

138

Practice Book - Section 8: Summary of Functions

5. Sketch an example of an even polynomial function below.

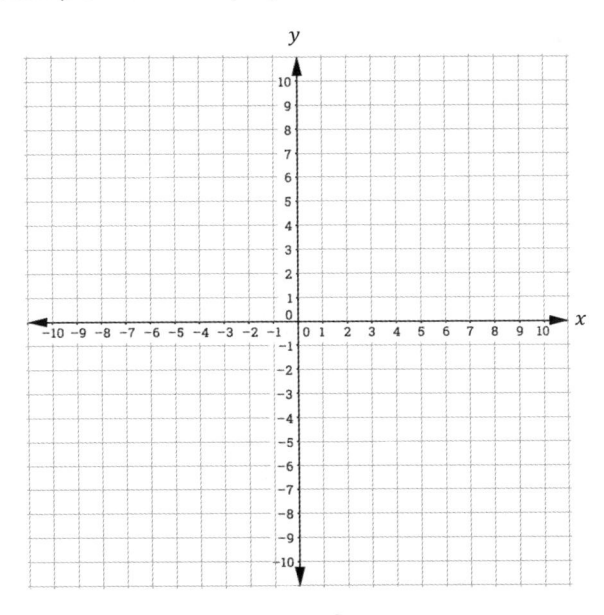

6. Sketch an example of an odd polynomial function below.

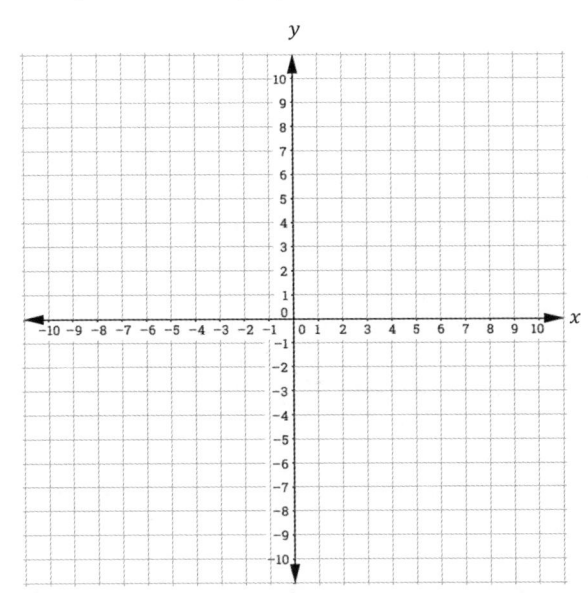

7. Sketch an example of a function that is neither even nor odd below.

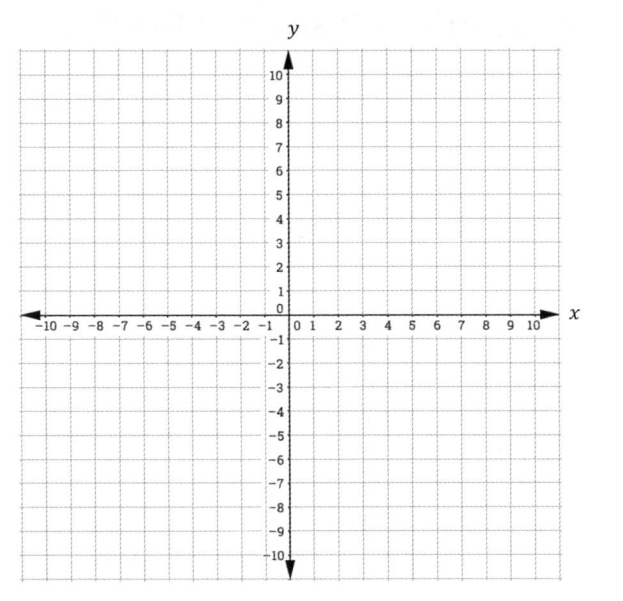

Practice Book - Section 8: Summary of Functions

Section 8 – Topic 14
Solutions to Systems of Functions

1. Consider the cubic function $f(x) = x^3$ and the absolute value function $h(x) = |x|$.

   Part A: Complete the table below.

x	$f(x)$	$h(x)$
-2		
-1		
0		
1		
2		

   Part B: At what value(s) for x does $f(x) = h(x)$?

2. Given the graphs of the exponential function $f(x) = 2^x - 6$ and the absolute value function, $g(x) = |x| - 1$, find the coordinate where $f(x) = g(x)$.

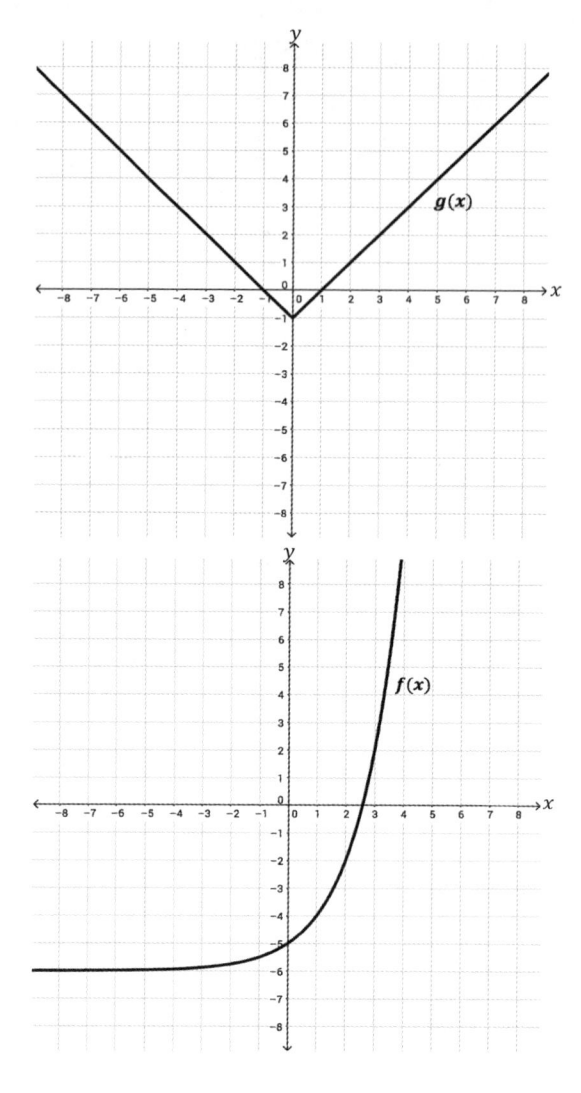

3. The graphs of the exponential function $m(x) = 3^x$ and the quadratic function $n(x) = -2x^2 + x + 4$ are shown on the same coordinate plane below.

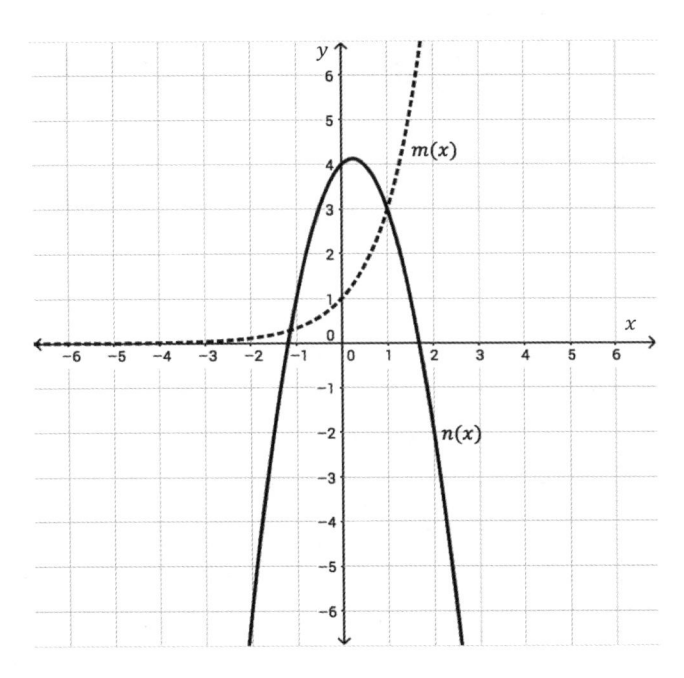

Which answer choice represents the coordinates where $m(x) = n(x)$?

Ⓐ $(1.7, 0)$ and $(-1.2, 0)$

Ⓑ $(-1.14, 0.29)$ and $(1, 3)$

Ⓒ $(0, 4)$ and $(-1, 0)$

Ⓓ $(-1, 3)$ and $(0.3, 4.2)$

4. Two swimmers jump from 12-foot diving boards. On the graph below, Swimmer 1's distance from the water is modeled by the function $f(x)$ and Swimmer 2's distance from the water is modeled by the function $g(x)$, where x represents time, in seconds.

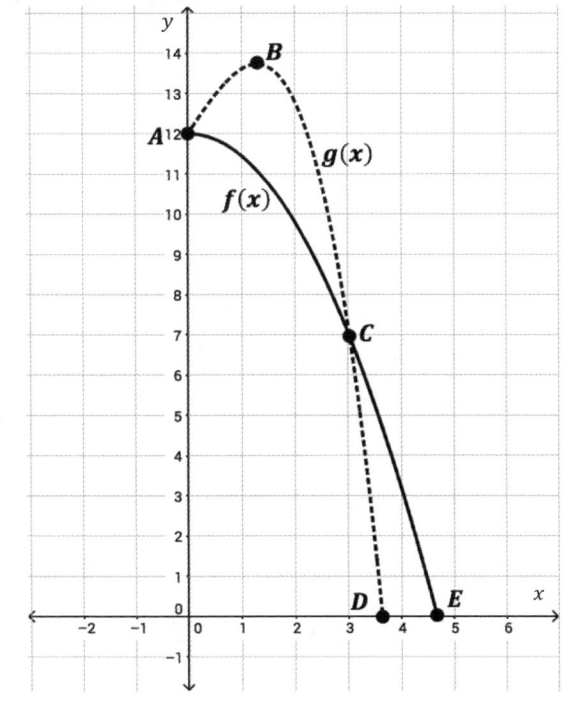

Part A: At which point(s) does $f(x) = g(x)$? Select all that apply.

☐ A
☐ B
☐ C
☐ D
☐ E

Part B: What does each point you selected in *Part A* represent in the context of this situation?

Part C: How is the domain for each function restricted? Why do you think that is?

Practice Book - Section 8: Summary of Functions

Section 9: One-Variable Statistics
Student Learning Plan

Topic Number	Topic Name	Date Completed	Study Expert(s)	Check Your Understanding Score
1	Dot Plots			
2	Histograms			
3	Box Plots – Part 1			
4	Box Plots – Part 2			
5	Measures of Center and Shapes of Distributions			
6	Measures of Spread – Part 1			
7	Measures of Spread – Part 2			
8	The Empirical Rule			
9	Outliers in Data Sets			
Honors 1	Normal Distribution			

*Honors resources are available online.

What did you learn in this section? What questions do you still have?

Who was your favorite Study Expert for this section? Why?

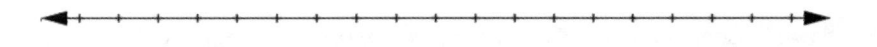

Section 9 – Topic 1
Dot Plots

1. The number of boots that 25 students had in their homes in Florida were recorded below:

   0, 0, 0, 0, 0, 0, 0, 1, 1, 1, 1, 2, 2, 2, 2, 2, 2, 2, 3, 3, 3, 3, 4, 5, 8

   Create a dot plot of the data above.

2. Classify the following variables as C – categorical, DQ – discrete quantitative, or CQ – continuous quantitative.

   _____ Distance that a golf ball was hit
   _____ Size of shoe
   _____ Favorite ice cream
   _____ Favorite number
   _____ Number of homework problems

3. Students in Ms. Multifry's class were surveyed about the number of pets they have. Their responses were recorded below:

   0, 0, 0, 0, 1, 1, 1, 1, 1, 1, 2, 2, 2, 2, 3, 3, 8

   Part A: Construct a dot plot of the data.

   Part B: What observations can you make about the shape of the distribution?

   Part C: Are there any values that seem to not fit?

4. Select the sets of data where it would be better to use a dot plot than a histogram.

   ☐ Average rainfall for Miami over a year
   ☐ Daily rainfall in Miami over a month
   ☐ Weight of patients in a doctor's office over a year
   ☐ Weight of students in your class
   ☐ Number of siblings each student in your math class has

5. The track team groups students based on times for a 100-meter dash, rounded to the nearest tenth of a second. The groups are as follows:

   Team A: 15 seconds or higher
   Team B: 11 - 14.9 seconds
   Team C: 10.9 seconds or lower

   Each track member's time has been recorded below.

   16.0, 14.9, 13.2, 12.5, 9.1, 8.1, 10.4, 10.8,
   8.4, 9.5, 9.5, 11.5, 15, 8.0, 9.7, 13.2, 12.1, 11.2

   Explain why a dot plot is not the best option to represent the data.

6. The amount of time 24 seniors spent at work in a given week is recorded as follows.

   | 19 | 12 | 12 | 8 | 19 | 4 | 5 | 4 | 7 | 0 | 3 | 0 |
   | 3 | 5 | 8 | 7 | 11 | 15 | 12 | 8 | 4 | 15 | 5 | 19 |

   Create a dot plot of the data above.

Section 9 – Topic 2
Histograms

1. The number of boots that 25 students had in their homes in Florida were recorded below:

   0, 0, 0, 0, 0, 0, 0, 1, 1, 1, 1, 2, 2, 2, 2, 2, 2, 2, 3, 3, 3, 3, 4, 5, 8

   Construct a histogram to represent the data.

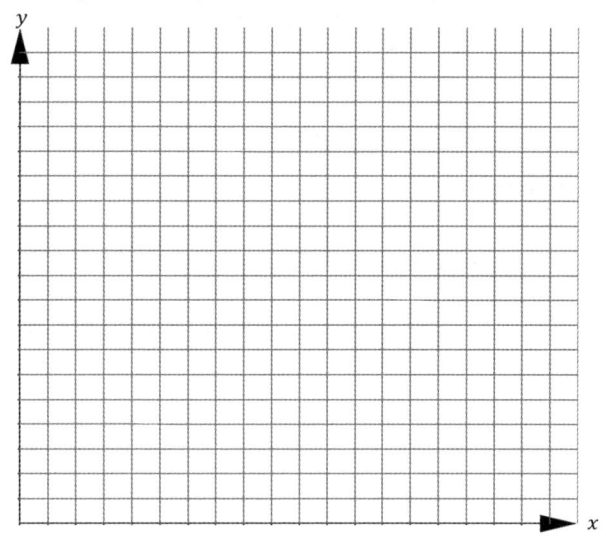

2. Select the sets of data where it would be better to use a histogram than a dot plot.

   ☐ Average rainfall for Miami over a year
   ☐ Daily rainfall in Miami over a month
   ☐ Weight of patients in a doctor's office over a year
   ☐ Weight of students in your class
   ☐ Number of siblings each student in your math class has

3. Students in Ms. Multifry's class were surveyed about the number of pets they have. Their responses were recorded below:

   0, 0, 0, 0, 1, 1, 1, 1, 1, 1, 2, 2, 2, 2, 3, 3, 8

   Part A: Describe why a histogram would be used for the data.

   Part B: Construct a histogram of the data.

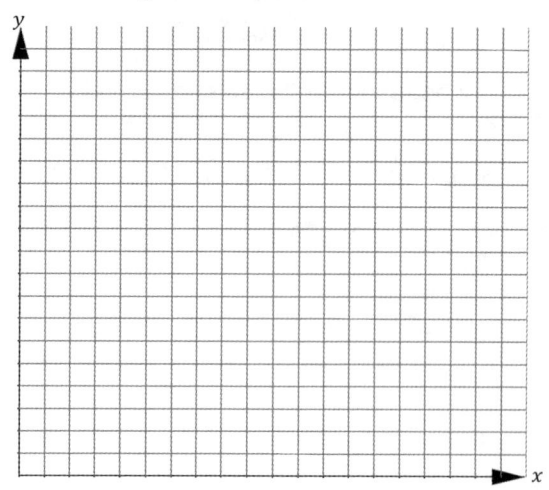

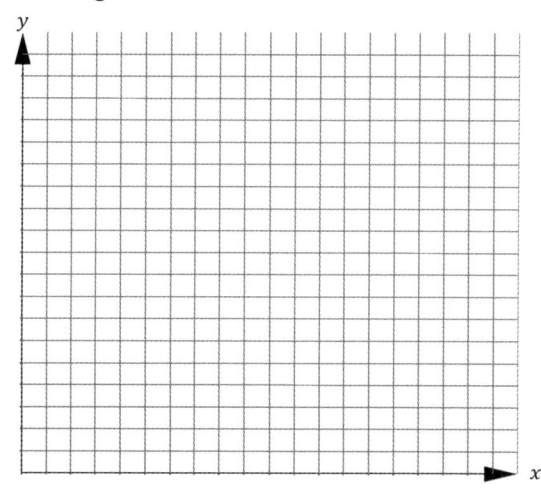

4. Last year, an intramural touch football team at the local university had a decent season. The total points scored by the team for each of the 20 games are listed below.

   | 24 | 28 | 34 | 36 | 36 | 40 | 41 | 43 | 43 | 48 |
   | 49 | 50 | 51 | 52 | 52 | 62 | 67 | 68 | 73 | 79 |

   Construct a histogram of the data.

5. The track team groups students based on times for a 100-meter dash, rounded to the nearest tenth of a second. The groups are as follows:

   Team A: 0-4.9 seconds
   Team B: 5-9.9 seconds
   Team C: 10-14.9 seconds
   Team D: 15-19.9 seconds

   Each track member's time has been recorded below.

   16.0, 14.9, 13.2, 12.5, 9.1, 8.1, 10.4, 10.8,
   8.4, 9.5, 9.5, 11.5, 15, 8.0, 9.7, 13.2, 12.1, 11.2

   Part A: Explain why a histogram would be a better representation model of the data.

   Part B: Complete the frequency table below:

Time (in seconds)	Frequency
Team A: 0-4.9 seconds	
Team B: 5-9.9 seconds	
Team C: 10-14.9 seconds	
Team D: 15-19.9 seconds	

   Part C: Construct a histogram of the data.

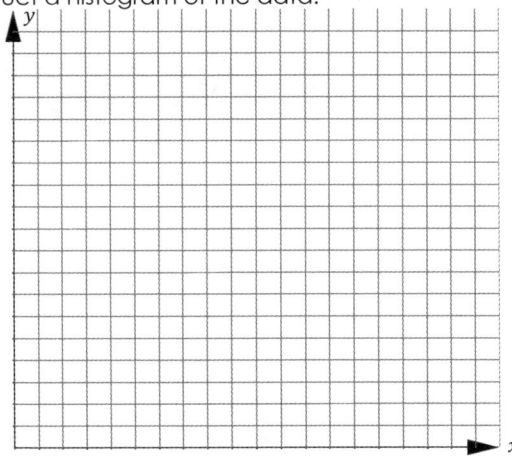

6. Below are the mountain heights for some mountains that are taller than 14,000 feet.

Name	Height (ft.)
Mt. McKinley	20,320
Mt. St. Elias	18,008
Mt. Foraker	17,400
Mt. Bona	16,500
Mt. Blackburn	16,390
Mt. Sanford	16,237
Mt. Vancouver	15,979
South Buttress	15,885
Mt. Churchill	15,638
Mt. Fairweather	15,300

Part A: Complete the frequency table below. You do not need to use all of the rows.

Mountain Height	Frequency

Part B: Construct a histogram of the data.

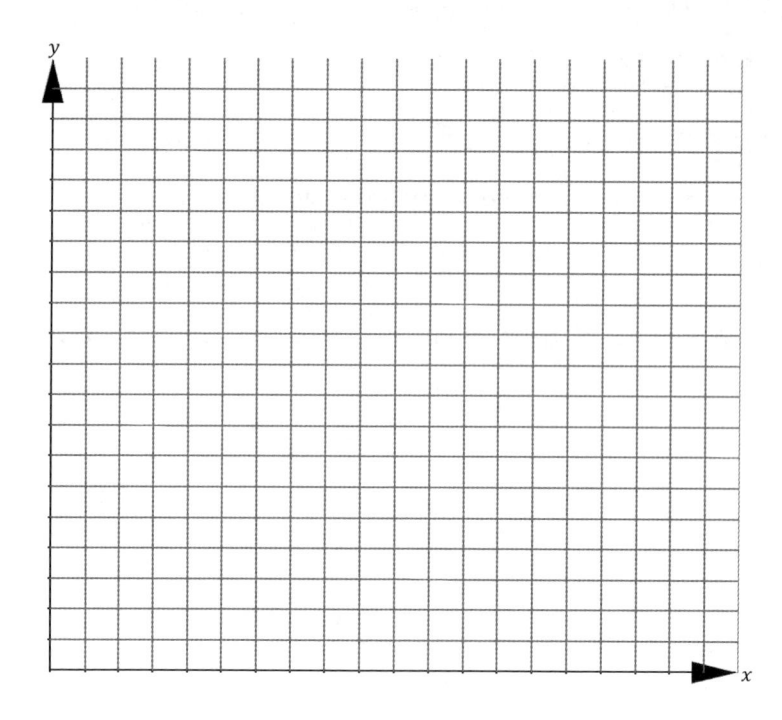

Section 9 – Topic 3
Box Plots – Part 1

1. Match the following elements of the 5-number survey to their corresponding descriptions.

_____	Minimum	**A.** Represents the lower 25% of the data.
_____	Maximum	**B.** The middle data value when the data is ordered least to greatest.
_____	First Quartile	**C.** The largest data value.
_____	Third Quartile	**D.** Represents the first 75% of the data.
_____	Median	**E.** The smallest data value.

2. Jason plays basketball for the Tigers, his high school basketball team. He played in 9 games during the season before he was hurt. The data set below represents the number of baskets he earned in each game.
$$16, 18, 20, 14, 17, 27, 33, 9, 12$$

Part A: Order the data from least to greatest.

Part B: Complete the following.

   a. The minimum value of the data set is:_____

   b. The maximum value of the data set is:_____

   c. The median of the data set is:_____

   d. The first quartile of the data set is:_____

   e. The third quartile of the data set is:_____

Part C: Graph the data by creating a box plot below.

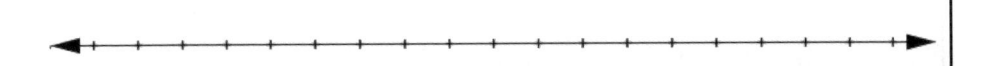

Part D: Interpret the data.

   a. What does the first quartile represent?

   b. What does the third quartile represent?

3. The following data displays the lengths of some rivers in the United States.
   - **Mississippi:** 2,340 miles
   - **Yukon:** 1,980 miles
   - **Rio Grande:** 1,900 miles
   - **Arkansas:** 1,460 miles
   - **Colorado:** 1,450 miles
   - **Ohio:** 1,310 miles
   - **Red:** 1,290 miles
   - **Brazos:** 1,280 miles
   - **Columbia:** 1,240 miles
   - **Snake:** 1,040 miles
   - **Platte:** 990 miles
   - **Pecos:** 926 miles

Part A: Create a box plot of the data above. Label the minimum, maximum, first quartile, third quartiles, and median.

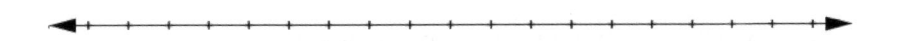

Part B: Name the rivers that make up the lower quartile.

Section 9 – Topic 4
Box Plots – Part 2

1. The number of boots that 25 students had in their homes in Florida were recorded below.
   0, 0, 0, 0, 0, 0, 0, 1, 1, 1, 1, 2, 2, 2, 2, 2, 2, 2, 3, 3, 3, 3, 4, 5, 6

   Create a box plot of the data above. Label the minimum, maximum, first quartile, third quartiles, and median.

2. One of the student's data was removed from the survey and replaced with a different student's data.
   0, 0, 0, 0, 0, 0, 0, 1, 1, 1, 1, 2, 2, 2, 2, 2, 2, 2, 3, 3, 3, 3, 4, 5, 9

   Create a box plot of the data above. Label the minimum, maximum, first quartile, third quartiles, and median.

3. Compare the five-number summaries in Questions 1 and 2. Which of the five-number summaries changed?

4. When the maximum value in a data set is exchanged for a higher number, does it change any of the other numbers in the five-number summary?

5. The box plot below represents the number of texts sent in two minutes by 11 different freshmen.

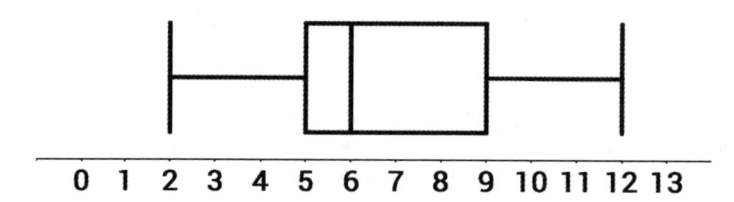

   Part A: The 75th percentile of the data set is _____.

   Part B: The middle half of the data values are between _____ and _____.

   Part C: 25% of the students sent _____ or fewer texts in two minutes.

6. Add dots to the number line below to complete the dot plot so that it could represent the data in the box plot in Question 5.

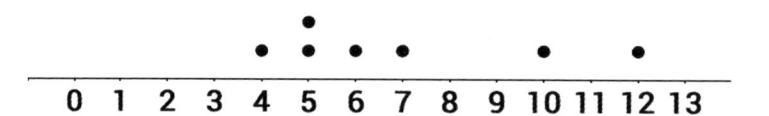

7. Determine whether the following statements are always, sometimes, or never true. Give examples to support your claim.

   Part A: Replacing only the minimum value in a data set with a smaller number will also change the median.

   Part B: Replacing only the minimum value in a data set with a smaller number will also change the mean.

   Part C: Replacing the maximum value of the data set with a smaller number will also change the median.

   Part D: Replacing the maximum value of the data set with a smaller number will also change the mean.

Section 9 – Topic 5
Measures of Center and Shapes of Distribution

1. Below is a dot plot of the number of Snapchats sent per day in Mr. Elkins' class.

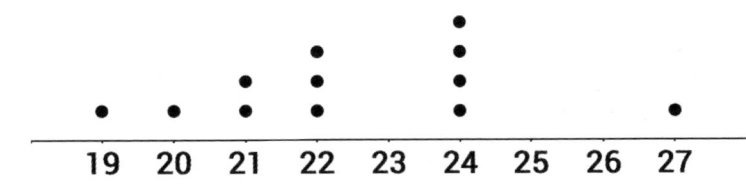

   Part A: Which value is smaller, the mean or the median?

   Part B: Which measure of center is more appropriate, the mean or the median?

   Part C: The shape of the distributions is _____.

2. Below is a dot plot of the number of concerts students in class have seen.

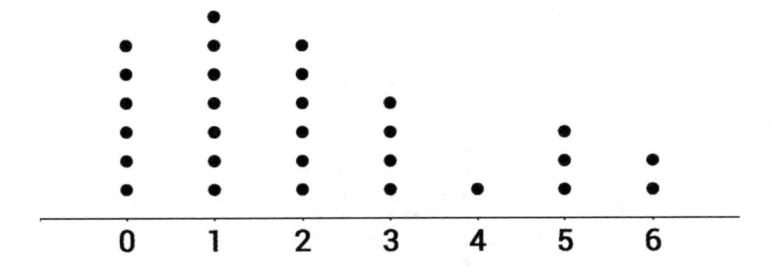

   Part A: Which value is smaller, the mean or the median?

   Part B: Which measure of center is more appropriate, the mean or the median? Why?

Part C: The shape of the distributions is _____.

3. Consider the dot plot below.

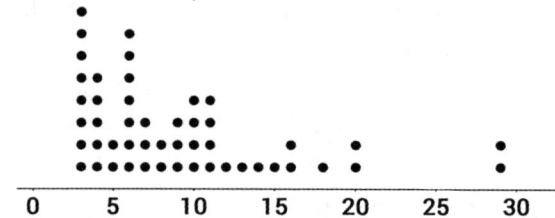

Part A: Which value is smaller, the mean or the median?

Part B: Which measure of center is more appropriate, the mean or the median?

Part C: The shape of the distribution is _____.

4. Below is a dot plot of the ages of the residents of Cypress Village Retirement Community.

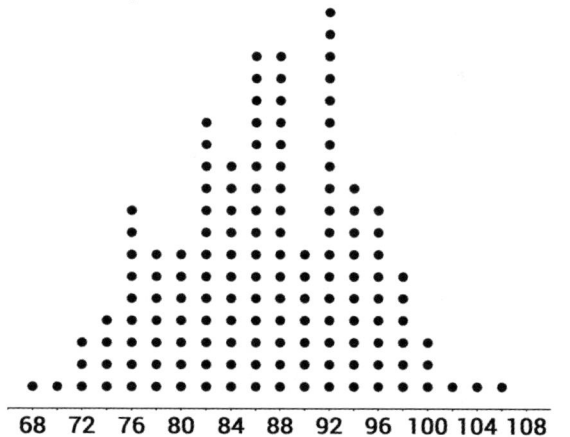

Part A: Looking at the dot plot, what is the value of the median?

Part B: What is the value of the mean?

Part C: Why is it important to know where the measure of center is?

Part D: The shape of the distribution is _____.

5. Below are two dot plots on students' moods during recess inside and outside. Their mood was recorded on a score of 0-10, 0 being depressed and 10 being excited.

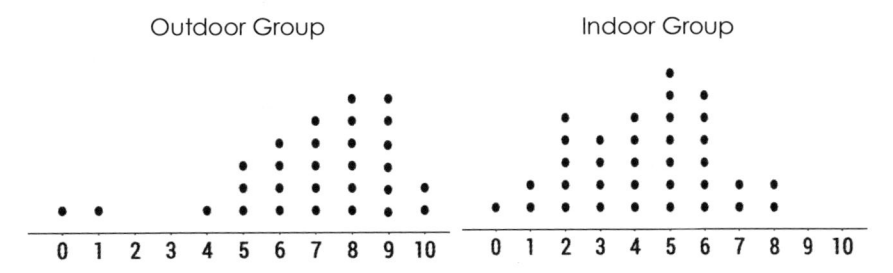

Outdoor Group   Indoor Group

Part A: The value of the larger median for the two groups is the _____.

Part B: The value of the larger mean for the two groups is the _____.

Part C: Describe the difference between the moods of the two groups by comparing their center and shapes for their groups.

6. Which of the following would you predict to be normally distributed? Check all that apply.

   ☐ The heights of men in the United States
   ☐ Data with a median greater than the mean
   ☐ Data with the exact same mean and median
   ☐ A dot plot with a peak in the middle of the data
   ☐ A dot plot with the most data values to the left of the peak

7. Below is a dot plot of the number of students in each math class at Lincoln Park Academy.

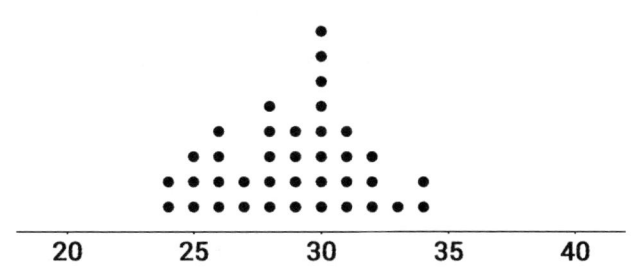

Part A: Looking at the dot plot, what is the value of the median?

Part B: What is the value of the mean?

Part C: Why do you think the values are so close to each other?

Practice Book - Section 9: One-Variable Statistics

Section 9 – Topic 6
Measures of Spread – Part 1

1. Below are dot plots of the number of chocolate chips in two different store brand cookies.

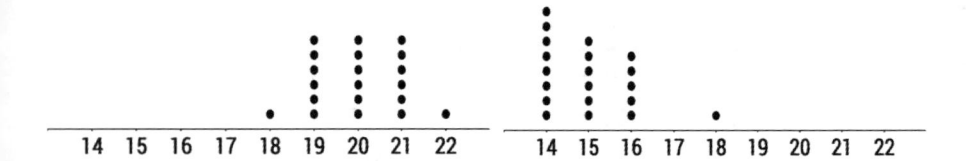

   Which data set has a larger standard deviation? Explain.

2. Consider the two box plots.

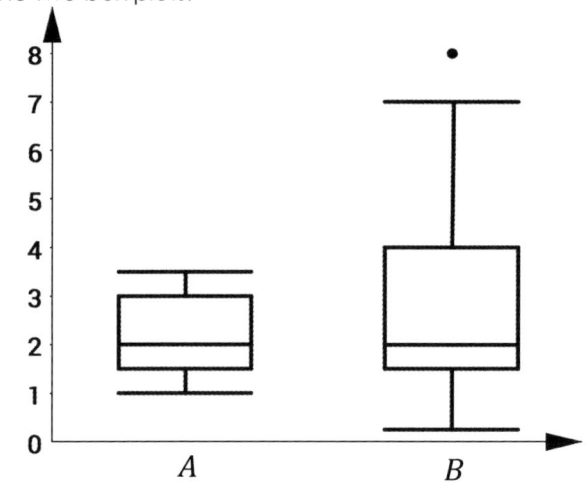

   Which has the largest IQR? Justify your answer.

3. Consider the following three box plots.

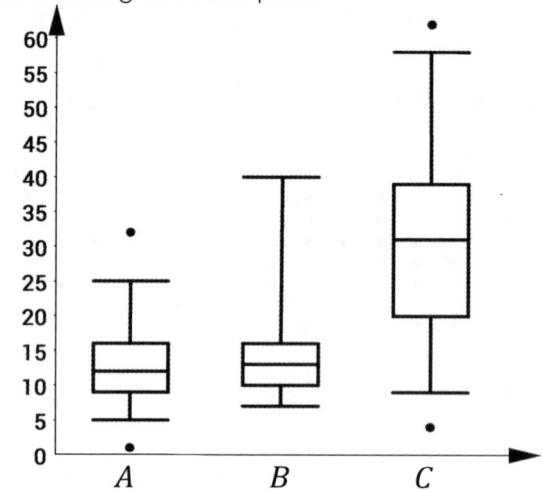

   Part A: Which has the largest median?

   Part B: Which has the largest IQR?

4. Below are the most recent quiz scores from Ms. Dillon's algebra class.

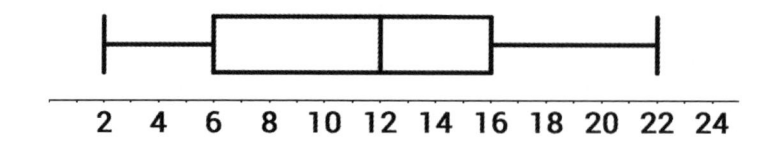

   Part A: What is the median of the algebra class?

   Part B: Determine the interquartile range.

Practice Book - Section 9: One-Variable Statistics

5. Consider the box plot below.

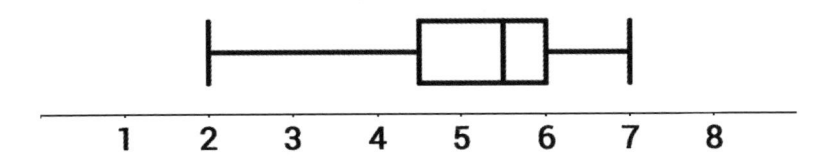

Part A: What is the median of the box plot?

Part B: Determine the interquartile range.

Section 9 – Topic 7
Measures of Spread – Part 2

1. Consider the two box plots.

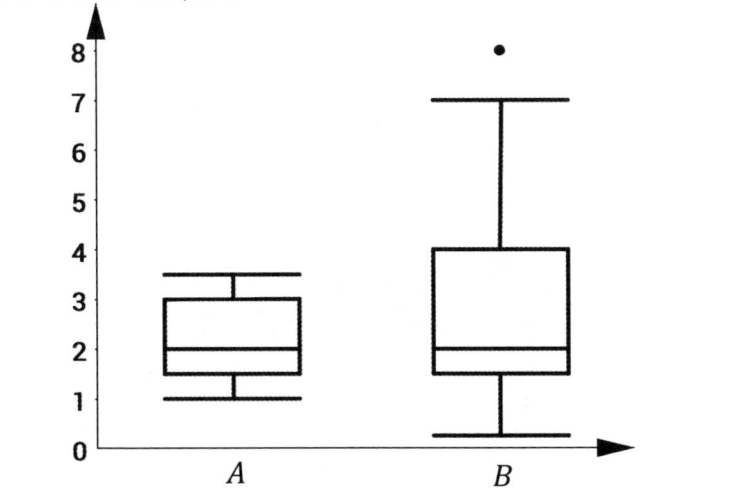

   Part A: Above are box plots that represent _____ for two different _____.

   Part B: Describe the shape of each distribution.

   Group A:

   Group B:

   Part C: Which has the largest median?

Practice Book - Section 9: One-Variable Statistics

2. Consider the following three box plots.

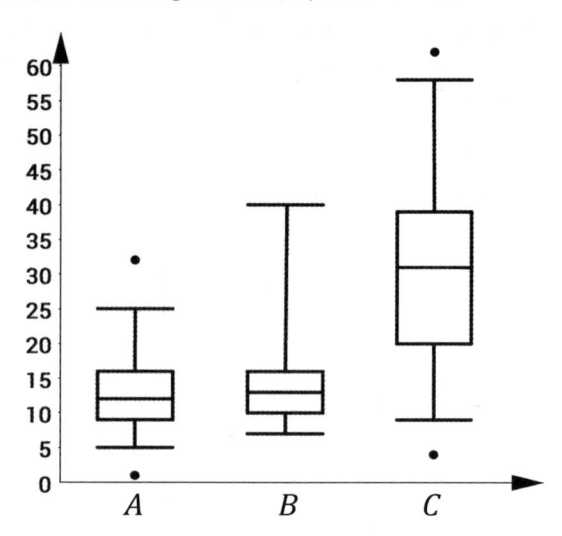

Describe the shape of each distribution.

Group A:

Group B:

Group C:

3. Below are the most recent quiz scores from Ms. Dillon's algebra class.

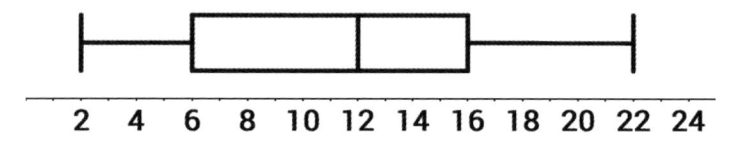

Part A: For the above box plot, would the mean or the median be the appropriate measure of center to describe the data distribution? Why?

Part B: Would the interquartile range or the standard deviation be the most appropriate measure of spread? Why?

Part C: Calculate the measure of spread.

4. Consider the box plot below.

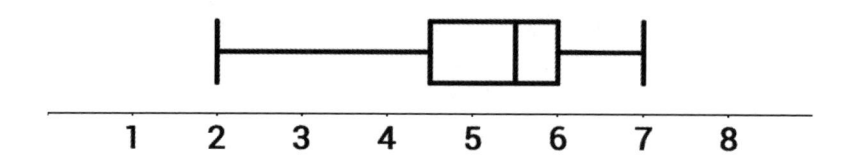

Part A: Would the mean or the median be the appropriate measure of center to describe the data distribution? Why?

Part A: Would the interquartile range or the standard deviation be the appropriate measure to describe the spread? Why?

Part B: Calculate the measure of spread.

Practice Book - Section 9: One-Variable Statistics

Section 9 – Topic 8
The Empirical Rule

1. Kellogg's in Kalamazoo, Michigan has a machine that fills the Fruit Loop cereal boxes with cereal. It dispenses cereal with a normal distribution and has a mean of 24.0 and a standard deviation of .1 ounces.

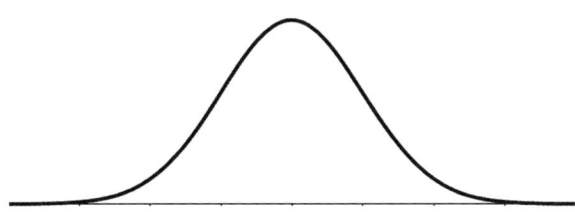

   Part A: The middle 95% of cereal boxes contain between _____ and _____ ounces of cereal.

   Part B: Approximately 68% of cereal boxes have between _____ and _____ ounces of cereal.

   Part C: What percentage of cereal boxes contain more than 24.2 ounces of cereal?

   Part D: What is the probability that a randomly selected box of cereal contains less than 24.1 ounces of cereal?

2. ACT mathematics scores for a particular year are normally distributed with a mean of 27 points and a standard deviation of 2 points.

   Part A: What is the probability that a randomly selected score is greater than 29 points?

   Part B: What percentage of students' scores are between 31 and 23?

   Part C: A student who scores a 31 is in the _____ percentile.

3. Mr. Barnett's test is normally distributed with a mean of 65 points and a standard deviation of 5 points.

   Part A: What is the probability that a randomly selected score is greater than 75 points?

   Part B: What percentage of students' scores are between 60 and 70?

   Part C: A student who scores an 80 is in the _____ percentile.

4. The number of times per minute that a hummingbird's wings flap is normally distributed with a mean of 145 times per minute and a standard deviation of 2 times per minute.

   Part A: What is the probability that a randomly selected hummingbird flaps its wings more than 151 times a minute?

   Part B: What percentage of hummingbirds flap their wings between 141 and 149 times per minute?

   Part C: A hummingbird that flaps its wings 147 times a minute is in the _____ percentile.

Section 9 – Topic 9
Outliers in Data Sets

1. The number of boots that 25 students had in their homes in Florida were recorded below:

   0, 0, 0, 0, 0, 0, 0, 1, 1, 1, 1, 2, 2, 2, 2, 2, 2, 2, 3, 3, 3, 3, 4, 5, 9

   Part A: What value would you predict to be an outlier?

   Part B: How does the outlier affect the mean?

   Part C: How does the outlier affect the median?

   Part D: Which measure of center would best describe the data- the mean or the median?

   Part E: How does the outlier affect the standard deviation?

   Part F: How does the outlier affect the interquartile range?

   Part G: Which measure of spread would best describe the data- the standard deviation or the interquartile range?

2. Below are the average incomes for different education levels.

Income by Education Levels	Income 2015
High School Dropout	$23,492
Some College	$36,804
Associates Degree	$42,820
Bachelor's Degree	$56,432
Master's Degree	$72,824
Professional Degree	$91,220
Doctoral Degree	$87,448

Part A: What value would you predict to be an outlier?

Part B: How does the outlier affect the mean?

Part C: How does the outlier affect the median?

Part D: Which measure of center would best describe the data- the mean or the median?

Part E: How can an outlier affect the standard deviation?

Part F: How does the outlier affect the interquartile range?

Part G: Which measure of spread would best describe the data- the standard deviation or the interquartile range if there is an outlier?

3. The table below lists the top ten most populated cities in 2014.

Rank	City*	Population 2014
1	Tokyo, Japan	37,833,000
2	Delhi, India	24,953,000
3	Shanghai, China	22,991,000
4	Mexico City, Mexico	20,843,000
5	São Paulo, Brazil	20,831,000
6	Mumbai, India	20,741,000
7	Osaka, Japan	20,123,000
8	Beijing, China	19,520,000
9	New York/Newark, United States	18,591,000
10	Cairo, Egypt	18,419,000

Part A: What value would you predict to be an outlier?

Part B: How does the outlier affect the mean?

Part C: How does the outlier affect the median?

Part D: Which measure of center would best describe the data- the mean or the median?

Part E: How does the outlier affect the standard deviation?

Part F: How does the outlier affect the interquartile range?

Part G: Which measure of spread would best describe the data- the standard deviation or the interquartile range?

Section 10: Two-Variable Statistics
Student Learning Plan

Topic Number	Topic Name	Date Completed	Study Expert(s)	Check Your Understanding Score
1	Relationship between Two Categorical Variables – Marginal and Joint Relative Frequency – Part 1			
2	Relationship between Two Categorical Variables – Marginal and Joint Relative Frequency – Part 2			
3	Relationship between Two Categorical Variables – Conditional Relative Frequency			
4	Scatter Plots and Function Models			
5	Residuals and Residual Plots – Part 1			
6	Residuals and Residual Plots – Part 2			
7	Examining Correlation			

What did you learn in this section? What questions do you still have?

Who was your favorite Study Expert for this section? Why?

Section 10 – Topic 1
Relationship between Two Categorical Variables – Marginal and Joint Relative Frequency – Part 1

1. Members of Alachua District Choir were asked, when given the choice between Romanticism or Gothic style singing, which style they preferred to sing for state competition. The data was broken down by gender.

    48 males preferred Romanticism
    63 males preferred Gothic
    59 females preferred Romanticism
    62 females preferred Gothic

    Part A: Fill in and complete the following contingency table. Circle the largest joint frequency and put a box around the smallest marginal frequency.

    Alachua District Choir Singing Style Preference

	Romanticism	Gothic	Total
Males			
Females			
Total			

    Part B: Which style was preferred as the state competition piece and by what percentage?

    Part C: Which style was preferred the most by males?

    Part D: What frequency does 125/232 represent?

2. Family vacationers were surveyed in the Marion County Rest Area, I-75 Southbound. The families were asked about what and how they primarily listen to music in their family cars while on the road.

    Family Vacationers Radio or Streaming Music

	Pop	Country	Total
Radio	84	70	
Streaming Music	56	96	
Total			

    Part A: Compute the joint and marginal relative frequencies in the table.

    Part B: How many families listened to pop music on the radio?

    Part C: What percentage of families listened to country music?

    Part D: How many families were interviewed?

    Part E: Circle the numbers that represent joint frequencies.

Practice Book - Section 10: Two-Variable Statistics

Section 10 – Topic 2
Relationship between Two Categorical Variables – Marginal and Joint Relative Frequency – Part 2

1. Students from Sandalwood High School were asked, when given the choice between math or English, which class they preferred to take during first period. The data was broken down by gender:

   55 males preferred math
   52 males preferred English
   42 females preferred math
   51 females preferred English

   Part A: Fill in and complete the following contingency table. Circle the largest joint frequency and put a box around the smallest marginal frequency.

   Sandalwood High School Survey of Preferred First Period Class

	Math	English	Total
Males			
Females			
Total			

   Part B: Which subject was preferred as a first period class and by what percentage?

   Part C: Males preferred which subject more?

   Part D: What frequency does 103/200 represent?

2. Long haul truckers were recently surveyed at a rest area in Tallahassee, Florida. The truckers were asked about what and how they primarily listen to music in their trucks while on the road.

   Long Haul Truckers Music Preferences While Traveling

	Talk Radio	Music	Total
Loud Volume	21	14	
Soft Volume	63	77	
Total			

   Part A: Compute the joint and marginal relative frequencies in the table.

   Part B: How many truckers listened to talk radio at a soft volume?

   Part C: What percentage of truckers listened at a loud volume?

   Part D: How many truckers were interviewed?

   Part E: Circle which numbers represent the joint frequencies.

3. Consumer Reports recently followed up with a survey to its readers asking about political preferences and primary choice of mobile device.

There was a total of 11,214 Republican respondents. Of the 9,500 Democrats responding, 470 reported using a device not listed and 292 said they used a Windows phone. The total usage of Android devices recorded totaled 8,926; 3,921 of Android users were Republicans. Interestingly, there were an equal number of Apple and Android users reporting as Republicans. There were 4,528 Democrats using an Apple device. Only 2,672 of those surveyed reported as Independent, 51 said they used a Windows device and 428 said they used an Apple device. There were 3,652 total Windows device users surveyed.

Consumer Reports Survey of Political Preference and Preferred Mobile Device

	Democrat	Republican	Independent	Total
Apple				
Android				
Windows				
Other				
Total				

Part A: Complete the two-way frequency table above.

Part B: What is the joint relative frequency of Independents using Apple devices?

Part C: What is the marginal frequency for all Windows devices?

Part D: How many respondents were there to the survey?

Part E: Which political party had the most respondents?

Part F: List the largest marginal frequency.

Part G: List the smallest joint relative frequency.

Practice Book - Section 10: Two-Variable Statistics

Section 10 – Topic 3
Relationship between Two Categorical Variables – Conditional Relative Frequency

1. Consider the following chart from the Kirkman Road Veterinary Clinic's database.

Clients at Kirkman Road Veterinary Clinic

	Microchipped	Not Microchipped	Total
Feline	58	109	167
Canine	250	27	277
Total	308	136	444

Part A: Which kind of pet is more likely to be microchipped?

Part B: What percentage of cats are not microchipped?

Part C: What percentage of dogs are not microchipped?

Part D: Of the pets that are microchipped, what percentage are dogs?

Part E: Of the pets that are not microchipped, what percentage are cats?

2. Consider the following data from Dann Orthodontics.

Dann Orthodontics Patient Data

	Wisdom Teeth	No Wisdom Teeth	Total
No Braces	36	55	
Braces Recommended	134	67	
Total			

Part A: What percentage of patients were recommended for braces?

This is a _____ relative frequency.

Part B: What percentage of patients without wisdom teeth were not recommended for braces?

This is a _____ relative frequency.

Part C: What percentage of those with wisdom teeth were recommended to receive braces?

This is a _____ relative frequency.

Part D: Does there seem to be a relationship between the presence of wisdom teeth and the recommendation for braces? Justify your answer.

Section 10 – Topic 4
Scatter Plots and Function Models

1. Below is a table of values for number of pictures added each year to the Tampa Tribune's database since 2000.

Year (2000-2014)	Number of Pictures in Database
2000	350
2001	419
2002	417
2003	376
2004	431
2005	404
2006	410
2007	373
2008	309
2009	465
2010	410
2011	499
2012	489
2013	516
2014	471

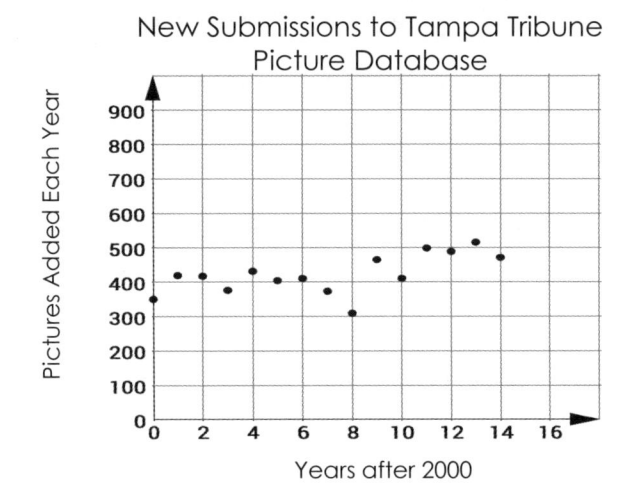

New Submissions to Tampa Tribune Picture Database

Part A: What do the values on the x-axis represent?

Part B: What do the values on the y-axis represent?

Part C: What does the value $(6, 410)$ represent?

Part D: Is the relationship positive, negative, zero or undetermined?

Part E: Is the correlation positive, negative, zero or undetermined?

Part F: Which of the following is closest to the regression line equation?

Ⓐ $f(x) = 366x + 8$
Ⓑ $f(x) = 13.4361(1.0079)^x$
Ⓒ $f(x) = 8x + 366$
Ⓓ None of the above is close enough

Part G: In approximately what year is the Tampa Tribune expecting to add 700 new pictures per year to their database?

Part H: James says that at some point the number of new pictures being added will begin to decrease. Does the data for the past 15 years support his hypothesis? Explain.

2. Match the following words to the scatter plots below. Each word may be used more than once.

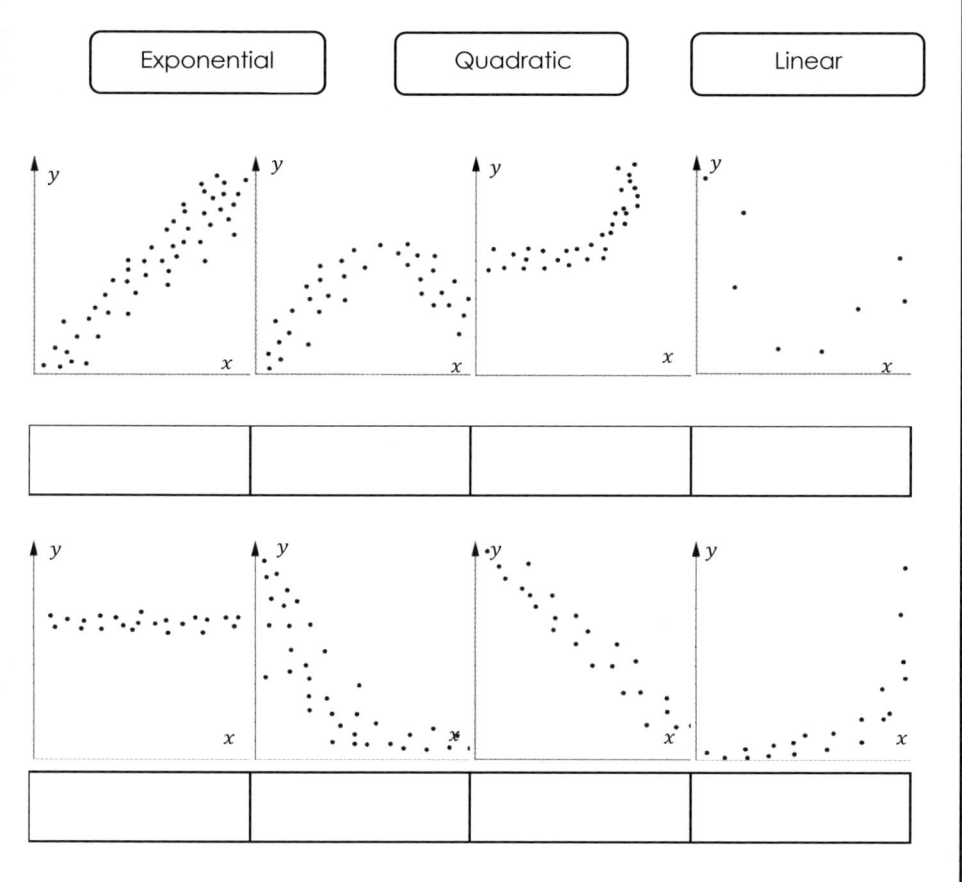

| Exponential | Quadratic | Linear |

3. When a movie is released to theaters, production companies monitor revenues from individual cities for that movie on its release date. Below is a table that shows 10 different movie revenues from opening night in both Tallahassee and Gainesville. Revenue is reported in millions of dollars.

| Tallahassee | 1.6 | 5.2 | 10.1 | 15.9 | 18.4 | 21.3 | 25.1 | 27.1 | 30.3 | 35.6 |
| Gainesville | 35.7 | 34.0 | 32.6 | 29.2 | 34.0 | 21.7 | 18.3 | 18.5 | 11.5 | 10.7 |

Part A: Represent the data on a scatter plot.

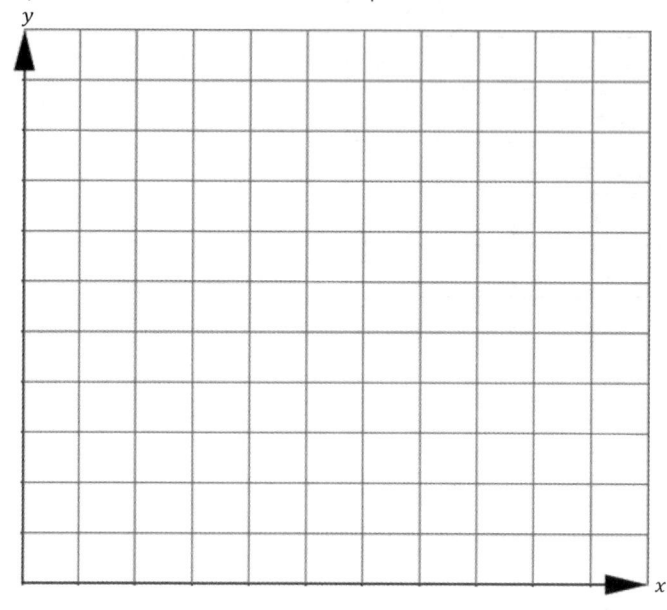

Part B: Which is the more appropriate function to model the data, where x represents the number of millions of dollars of revenue from Tallahassee theaters?

Ⓐ $f(x) = -0.805x + 38.967$
Ⓑ $f(x) = 0.805x + 38.967$
Ⓒ $f(x) = -0.001x^2 - 0.543x + 37.389$
Ⓓ $f(x) = 40.5(0.96)^x$

Part C: According to the model, if a movie brought in $32.2 million in total sales in Tallahassee, what would the expected sales be for Gainesville?

Part D: Sammy Nole predicted that if a movie brings in only $1.6 million in sales in Gainesville that the movie would bring in $35.7 million when shown in Tallahassee. Does the data support this hypothesis? Justify your answer.

Section 10 – Topic 5
Residuals and Residual Plots – Part 1

1. For each statement below, mark if it's TRUE or FALSE.

True	False	Statement
○	○	Residuals are calculated by finding the difference between the actual y-value and the predicted y-value.
○	○	Residuals should either be all positive or all negative.
○	○	Residual plots determine if a function is a good fit.
○	○	The sum of the residuals should always be 0 because the predicted values should be that close to the actual values.
○	○	When the best fit line for a set of data is quadratic, the residual will have no distinct pattern.

2. Beyoncé recently posted a new music video on Twitter at 4:00 am and the retweets were tracked per hour after the post. The times in hours are tracked below:

Hour	1	2	3	4	5	6	7	8
Retweets	65	90	162	224	377	466	780	1087

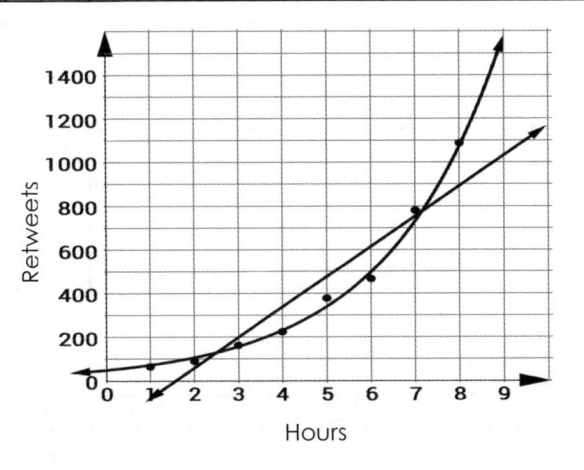

Practice Book - Section 10: Two-Variable Statistics

Part A: Which function should be used to fit the data? Circle one.
  Linear: $f(x) = 138.9x - 218.76$

  Exponential: $f(x) = 49.3(1.47)^x$

Part B: Complete the following table for residuals for the linear function $f(x) = 138.9x - 218.76$.

Hour	Retweets	Predicted Value	Residual
1	65		
2	90		
3	162		
4	224		
5	337		
6	466		
7	780		
8	1087		

Part C: Complete the following table for residuals for the exponential function $f(x) = 49.3(1.47)^x$.

Hour	Retweets	Predicted Value	Residual
1	65		
2	90		
3	162		
4	224		
5	337		
6	466		
7	780		
8	1087		

Part D: Which function had more alternating residual values?

Part E: Sketch the graph of the residual values of the linear model below.

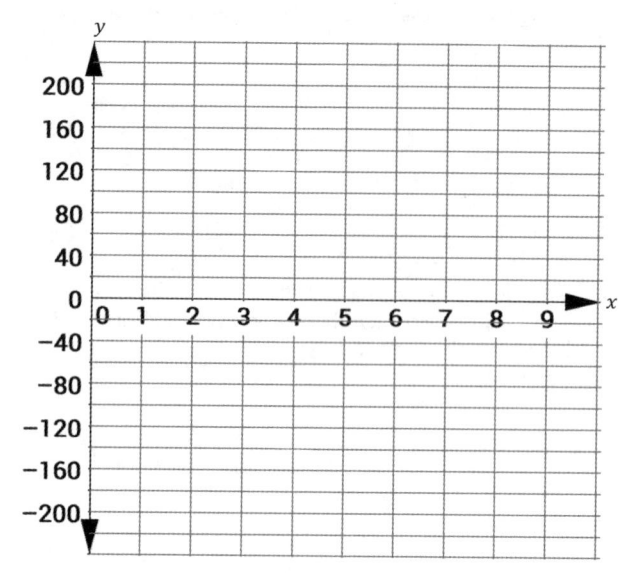

Part F: Graph the residual values of the exponential model below.

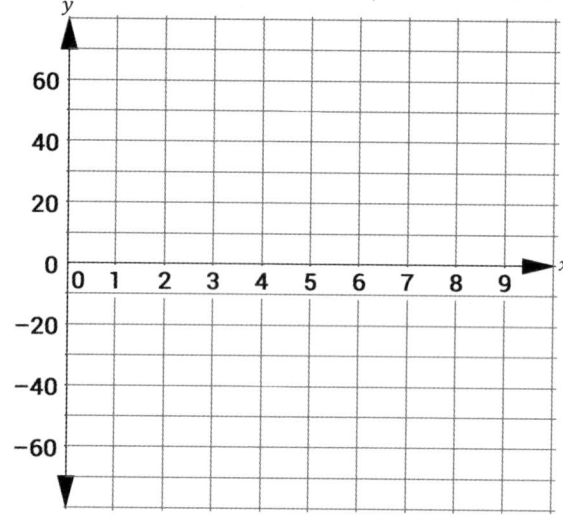

Part G: Which model most accurately represents the data? Justify your answer.

3. The following graphs have been collected from the residuals of scatter plots and their best fit lines. Circle all of the following that indicate that the data set has a line of best fit.

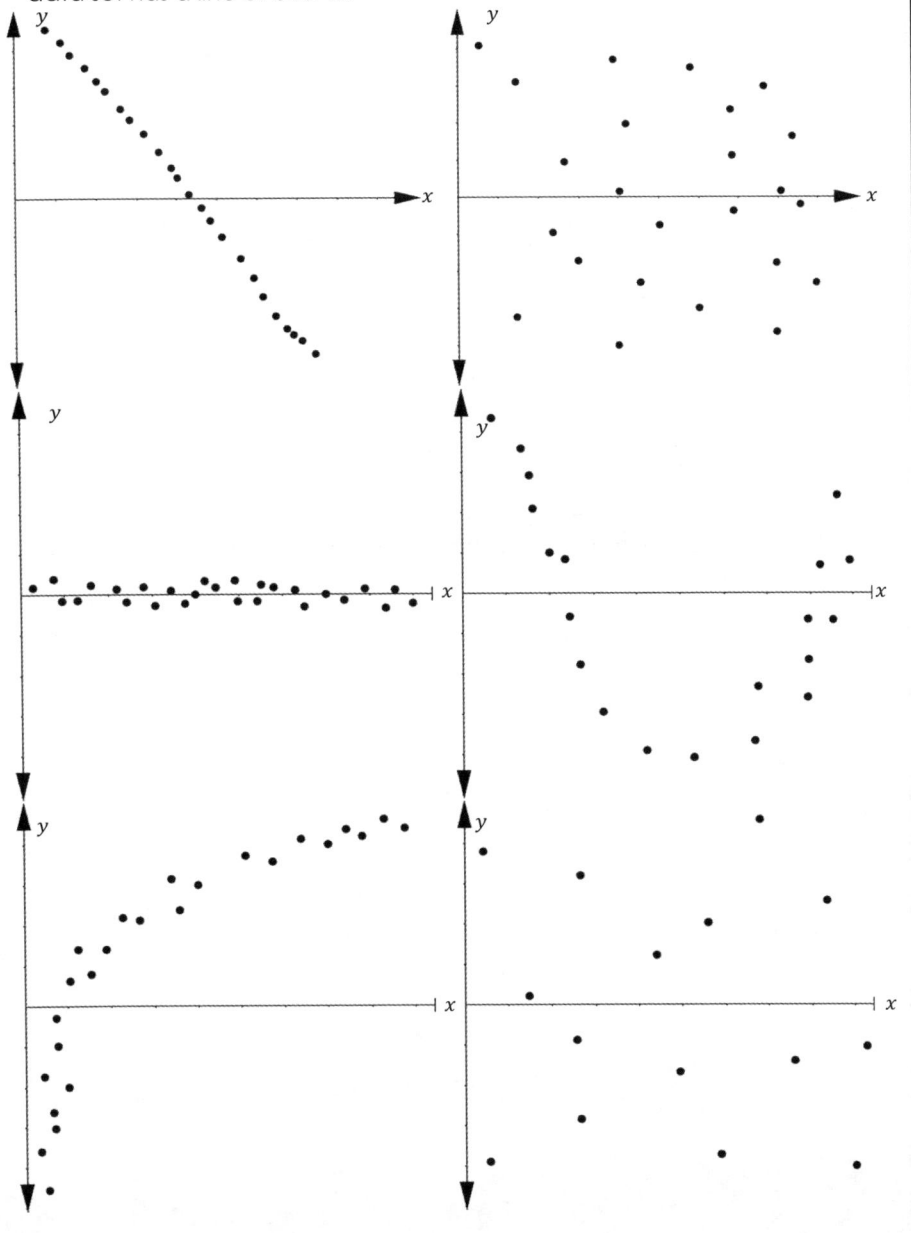

Section 10 – Topic 6
Residuals and Residual Plots – Part 2

1. If a data set has an exponential trend and a linear function is fit to the data, what will the residual plot look like?

2. Consider the residual plots shown below.

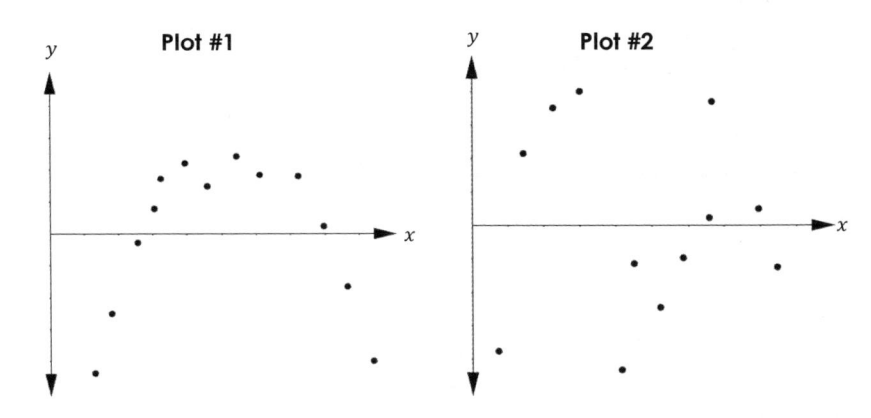

   Plot #1   Plot #2

   What is the difference between these residual plots?

3. A model was fit for a data set using linear regression. Residual plots for two data sets are shown below. Determine and justify which one could represent the data.

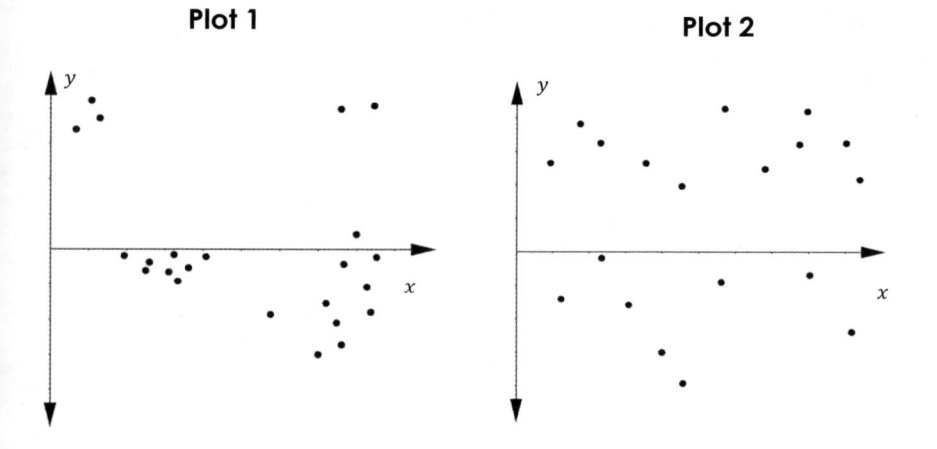

Plot 1

Plot 2

4. Consider the following residual plot.

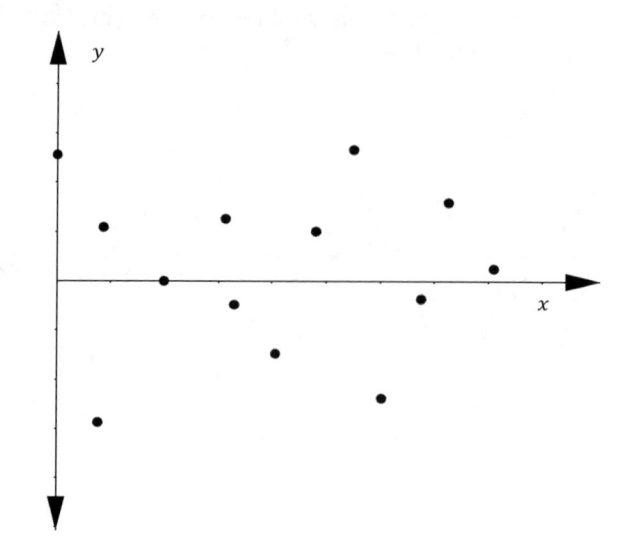

Part A: Does the residual plot show a good fit for the model that was used for the data?

Part B: Describe the model that was fitted to the data. Determine if the residual plot on the previous page could represent the data.

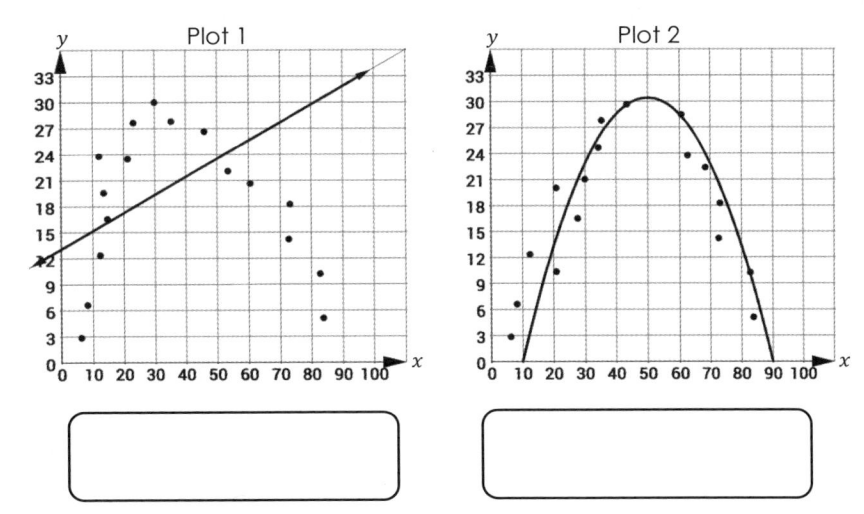

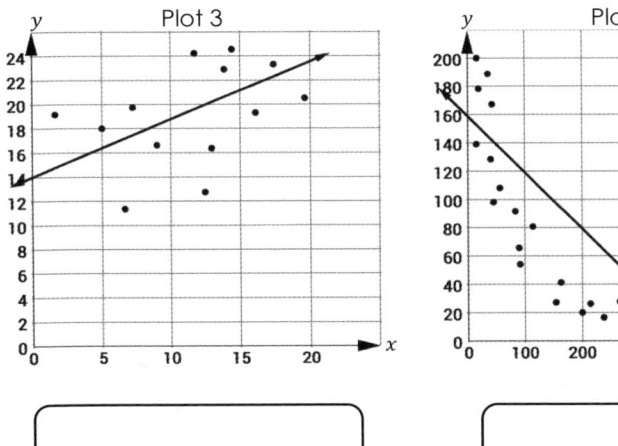

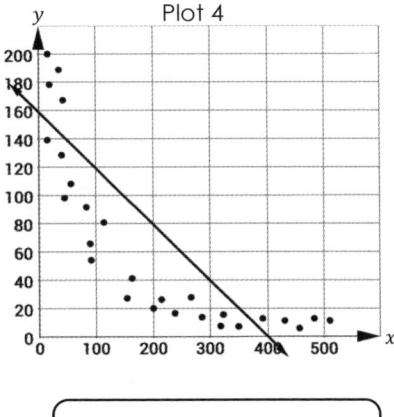

Plot 1

Plot 2

Plot 3

Plot 4

Section 10 – Topic 7
Examining Correlation

1. Select all of the following statements that are true.

   ☐ Correlation coefficients show the x and y intercepts of the best fit line.
   ☐ Correlation coefficients show the relationship of the x and y values.
   ☐ Correlation coefficients can be represented by the variable r.
   ☐ Correlation coefficients are negative when the relationship is weak and positive when the relationship is strong.
   ☐ Correlation coefficients can be any value less than 1 or greater than -1.

2. In your own words, what does an r value of -1 represent?

3. Circle the word that makes the statements correct.

   Correlation does | does not imply causation.

   Causation is when one event does | does not cause another event to happen.

   Two variables are always | sometimes | never correlated.

4. In the U.S., from 2004 – 2015, the correlation coefficient for the relationship between the size of a cell phone data plan, x, and the number of text messages sent, y, is $r = +0.97$. Describe the relationship between the data plan size and the number of text messages sent in the U.S.

Practice Book - Section 10: Two-Variable Statistics

Notes

Notes

Notes

Notes

Notes